EARTHQUAKE:

SURVIVING
The Big One

EARTHQUAKE:

SURVIVING
The Big One

BY
SUSAN MAYSE

LONE PINE

The Publisher:
Lone Pine Publishing
206, 10426 - 81 Avenue
Edmonton, Alberta, Canada
T6E 1X5

Canadian Cataloguing in Publication Data

Mayse, Susan, 1948-
    Earthquake: Surviving the Big One

    Includes index.
    ISBN 1-55105-003-X

    1. Earthquakes – Safety measures – Handbooks, manuals, etc. 2. Earthquakes – British Columbia – Greater Vancouver – Safety measures – Handbooks, manuals, etc. 3. Earthquakes – British Columbia – Vancouver Island – Safety measures – Handbooks, manuals, etc. I. Title.
    HV599.M39 1992   363.3′495′0971133   C92-091097-1

Cover Design: Beata Kurpinski
Editorial: Lloyd Dick, Gary Whyte
Design & Layout: Beata Kurpinski, Will Jang
Printing: Quality Color Press, Ltd.,Edmonton, Alberta

The publisher gratefully acknowledges the assistance of the Federal Department of Communicatons, Alberta Culture and Multiculuralism, the Canada Council, and the Alberta Foundation for the Arts in the production of this book.

CONTENTS

Photo Credits

British Columbia Provincial Emergency Program: p.69

F.A.S.T. Limited: p.78

Al Harvey: Cover

E.A. Hodgson,
courtesy of the Geological Survey of Canada at the
Pacific Geoscience Centre: p.38

E.A. Hodgson collection,
courtesy of the Geological Survey of Canada at the Pacific
Geoscience Centre: p.23

Stephen Hume: p.10

Edith Irvine,
courtesy Brigham Young University: pp.106 & 107

William Jones,
courtesy of the Geological Survey of Canada at the
Pacific Geoscience Centre: p.64

Bruce Stotesbury: pp.14 & 15

United States Geological Survey:
pp.12, 13, 18, .24, 27, 31, 33, 52, 85, 104, 142

Illustrations by Linda Dunn

Many people provided useful advice, information and insights as I researched earthquakes and their effects in coastal British Columbia. My special thanks to:

Mel Blaney, City of Vancouver

Harry and Dot Buchanan

members of Burkeville Emergency Response Team (BERT)

Krysha Derbyshire, North and West Vancouver Emergency Social Services

Doug Elliott, B.C. Telephone

Dave Gronbeck-Jones, Provincial Emergency Program

Ruth Harding, B.C. Telephone

Terry Jarvis, Cumberland Junior High School

Andrea Lacasse, City of Richmond

Carolyn and Rick Lloyd

Brad Lloyd

Donn Louie

Don MacIver, City of Richmond

Taimi Mulder, Geological Survey of Canada

Ross Peterson, North and West Vancouver Emergency Program

Bill Manery, B.C. Gas

John Oakley, City of Vancouver

Lynn Orstad, Canadian Red Cross

Doug Peterson, Greater Vancouver Regional District

Billy Plunkett, Brigham Young University

Dr. Garry Rogers, Geological Survey of Canada

Alex Stewart

Jeanette Taylor, Campbell River Museum

Robin Thoms, Emergency Preparedness Canada

Dr. Dieter Weichert, Geological Survey of Canada

U.S. Geological Survey
Canadian Geological Survey
Provincial Emergency Program, British Columbia
F.A.S.T., Limited
Al Harvey

INTRODUCTION
SURVIVOR'S GUILT

Earthquakes were minor excitement when I was growing up on Vancouver Island. The ground shook for a while, a few panes of glass broke, and maybe there was a piddling tidal wave. Seismologists assured us for years that the British Columbia coast was not seismically active. Then came a series of monster quakes along the west coast of North and South America, and the new theory of plate tectonics to explain why they were occurring and why we could expect more. By the early '90s, seismologists had a good idea that coastal British Columbia was not only highly seismic, but due for a major earthquake. We're still waiting for The Big One.

When I returned to live on the British Columbia coast, I wanted to know what to do for self-preservation in a big quake. A few magazine and newspaper stories offered good pointers, but I couldn't find a British Columbia based book on earthquake planning, preparation, survival and recovery. California, Japan and New Zealand abound in such information, but I soon discovered that they are decades ahead of Canada in earthquake awareness. And good advice for Nagoya or Auckland may not be suitable for Vancouver Island and the Lower Mainland. California information is more applicable because we are closer in lifestyle, building methods and geography, but the United States takes a different approach to every aspect of earthquakes. Obviously, British Columbians needed a handbook based on local conditions. The information was out there, largely in the hands of seismologists and emergency planning specialists, and was trickling out through the usual channels of media and community meetings. Still, it eluded the many people who don't regularly follow electronic or print media, and who don't attend community events. It was unavailable to people who wanted a single source of information that would cost less than a pizza and fit in a coat pocket, people like me. This book is a byproduct of the research I began for my own information.

INTRODUCTION

Shoppers and tourists enjoy Vancouver's Gastown district. Some of its historic masonry buildings on narrow streets have been retrofitted for seismic safety. Others could fall in a major quake, like heritage buildings elsewhere in British Columbia.

Writing about disaster planning and survival means walking a fine and unforgiving line: overstep on one side and stir alarmist overreaction, overstep on the other and encourage apathy. I lean toward alarmism, since my readings and interviews all confirm that a worst-case earthquake could have horrendous consequences. Your chances of surviving an earthquake are excellent and probably, as popular wisdom claims, better than your chances of surviving the daily drive to work. But survival is not the only goal. With a little preparation you can probably save not only yourself but your home, your personal property, your livelihood, and your most precious possession – peace of mind.

I've had personal experience with natural disaster during the years I spent in Edmonton. I lived through that city's devestating 1987 tornado, and spending the night curled up in an Edmonton basement stairwell with a flashlight and two cats gives one time to think about tornadoes, terror and the nature of the universe. One conclusion I reached in that meditative state was that, on the whole, I'd rather be back home in earthquake country.

Survivor's guilt is insidious. Although the house never blew apart around us, we did drive through the black heart of tornadoes on two separate occasions. If you're caught on a prairie road in your car, there's not much else you can do. This, plus the experience of remaining unscathed while others were homeless or bereaved, had its effect. Like the Ancient Mariner, I developed a strong interest both in surviving and in writing about survival.

In researching and writing this book I've built on the experience of emergency preparedness planners as well as less conventional sources. Naturally I was seeking answers to my own questions about earthquake planning and survival. In time I also noticed a pattern in the questions people asked me about this project. Most people asked about the relative safety of different housing types, municipalities and neighbourhoods. Many asked how much food and water to have on hand. Some grasped the need to prepare, but wondered where to start. And, usually in the guise of a joke, some asked if they would fall into a fissure in the earth, sink into quicksand or be washed away by a tidal wave. All of their instincts were flawless. Shelter, food and water are vital concerns, but fears of earth crumbling underfoot or of wild rising seas are pure nightmare material, the substance of our deepest and oldest terrors. People need to know the answers to these questions to feel safe and to make themselves safer.

Most difficult to research and convincingly portray is the reality of a great earthquake in British Columbia, and the devastation it will cause in every phase of our lives. We're living dangerously, whether or not we realize it. The last time a monster quake probably occurred here several hundred years ago, aboriginal peoples were living in one-storey cedar plank houses near their fishing grounds. True, they had to worry about tidal waves, landslides, falling trees, fires, and the abrupt lowering or raising of sea levels; they didn't have to also worry about being electrocuted, trapped under a collapsed freeway, buried two metres deep in broken glass from downtown office towers or other lethal hazards peculiar to 20th century life.

Earthquake: Surviving The Big One is for people who want to prepare themselves, their homes and their small businesses to withstand a major earthquake. It cannot replace the professional guidance of engineers, consultants, counsellors and others. It can only offer advice. In the end, the choice of how to proceed is yours. You can make a full-time job and spend a modest fortune in earthquake preparation; if that approach reassures or entertains you, go right ahead. Or you can draw the line at a spare toothbrush and a quarter for a pay phone. You alone know how fully you want, need and can afford to prepare. Any special cir-

Hospitals provide essential treatment for earthquake victims who may number in the thousands as well as maintaining services to present patients. Thus the loss of a hospital is a double tragedy. The maternity wing of Juarez Hospital in Mexico City collapsed in the September 1985 quake, trapping 400 staff members an patients. Rescuers tunnelled through debris to rescue survivors up to 10 days after the quake.

cumstances – such as the presence of elderly, very young, or physically or mentally challenged people – will naturally guide your decision.

However thoroughly you prepare, it's still possible that you will lose your home and all that's in it, all the treasures and trivia of a lifetime. No one can predict exactly what damage will result from an anticipated large quake. Two quakes of the same magnitude but different duration, for example, could have quite different effects. One might crack your windows and rearrange your china cabinet; a second might shift your house off its foundations. The likelihood of total loss is small, but the prospect can help you to keep your personal values in sharp perspective. While people often do crackbrained things in a crisis – such as running back into a burning house for a chipped saucer – your rational priority will be human survival.

The best thing that could happen in British Columbia right now is a moderate earthquake to shake us awake, several emergency planners told me. Lynn Orstad of the Canadian Red Cross described it almost wistfully. "A small earthquake, about a five. No structural damage, just a little shake and a couple of pic-

Slumping and landslides can damage buildings, roads and other structures. The June 1946 B.C. quake damaged a Read Island farm's fields and orchards.

tures falling, and maybe one piece of china that means a lot to someone, breaking. No injuries, no deaths." Californians have the advantage of a moderate quake every few years to sharpen their skills and awareness. Here we need a reminder. Not only would we get serious about planning and preparation, but we'd get some useful experience in diving under desks and waiting for the shaking to stop.

Second best is a book like this. *Earthquake: Surviving The Big One* will help you prepare to survive what may be the most alarming – but interesting – event of your life.

- take family to mean group of people living together
- entire book is in effect extended family emergency plan
- guiding principles: recycle, revise, reduce
- everything you do will help you live more efficiently and safely, will wonder why you didn't do it before now

BEFORE

Victoria,
British Columbia

BEFORE

CHAPTER 1

ON SHAKY GROUND

Most people in British Columbia have never ridden out a major earthquake, yet scientists warn us that British Columbia's coastal regions, including the Lower Mainland and Vancouver Island, can expect a powerful quake. Canadian earthquake experts now believe there's a strong likelihood of a major earthquake occurring here within the next 200 years. It could strike in 200 years, or it could strike tomorrow.

The 1985 Mexico City quake shook us out of our official lethargy. Federal, provincial and local governments began serious planning for a large earthquake in British Columbia. All three have undertaken comprehensive earthquake response plans designed not only to mesh with each other but to provide for emergency assistance from Alberta and neighbouring states.

The October 1989 Loma Prieta quake near San Francisco awakened public awareness. We heard, watched, read and talked about earthquakes long after the last untelevised rescues, burials and demolitions.

California is British Columbia's near neighbour. Many Canadians have family ties there, and it's only hours away by air. Loma Prieta was the most serious earthquake in recent years to strike a country where people share our language, culture and lifestyle. It made a powerful impression.

Research in seismology (the study of earthquakes), vulcanology and the earth's crustal movements has intensified in the last decade, much of it by the Geological Survey of Canada at the Pacific Geoscience Centre near Sidney. Experts may disagree about the particulars, but many now speak of when – not if – The Big One will strike.

Severe damage, many casualties, and loss of services over a wide area are the prediction of a 1990 draft of British Columbia's provincial interim earthquake response plan. In addition to damage caused by ground shaking, there may also be landslides, flooding, tidal waves and fires.

Houses sometimes collapse after prolonged shaking, as this Boulder Creek, California house did in the Loma Prieta earthquake of October 1989. Even if a house remains on its foundations, a "soft storey" or insufficiently braced ground floor can collapse.

"The principal cause of deaths and injury will be the collapse of buildings and other manmade structures, particularly older, multi-storey, and unreinforced masonry buildings," the plan reports.

"Structures in these categories include many of our schools and hospitals, which are expected to suffer at least 50-per-cent uninhabitability due to partial or complete collapse."

An early draft of a federal government plan also predicts heavy damage in the Lower Mainland. A big quake could destroy or make uninhabitable 10 to 30 per cent of single-family housing, 50 to 100 per cent of unreinforced masonry buildings, 10 to 20 per cent of highrises, and up to 60 per cent of older schools and hospitals which have not been strengthened for earthquake resistance. Several recent hazard assessment studies have supported these conclusions.

Exactly when we can expect The Big One is unknown and probably unknowable. Seismologists speak in terms of probabilities over the next few centuries. Engineers restrict themselves to discussion of possible damage and its prevention. Only self-appointed instant experts and clairvoyants claim they can pinpoint earthquakes, and their success rate so far is uninspiring.

Their main effect, to the frustration of emergency planners who answer the scores of frantic telephone calls, is to cause a momen-tary flood of ill-informed panic and a long ebb of equally foolish indifference. But by then the overnight experts, having collected their speaking engagement fees, are notably silent.

Prediction capability is still severely limited, although seismologists hope someday to recognize patterns of fore-shocks as irrefutable warning of a major earthquake. Even in California, the focus of much research and discussion since the devastating 1906 San Francisco earthquake, the government's infrequent quake warnings and alerts now offer only a general indication of likely time and place. Other factors can affect accuracy, as in March 1991 when heavy rains triggered ground motion sensors in the Parkfield section of the San Andreas Fault, mimicking pre-earthquake ground motion.

All the recent interest in quakes is a good reminder of the practical reality: we need to prepare thoroughly right now to ride out a great quake.

WHAT HAPPENS

News features from around the world show us brickpiles that were once buildings, collapsed bridges, broken pavements, and related fire and flood damage. We cheer on rescue teams searching the ruins for survivors in television coverage from Mexico City and San Francisco. We marvel that a few seconds of shaking seem to produce worse damage than intensive high-explosives bombing. We learn that many thousands of unlocated bodies still lie in the wreckage of Leni-nakan and Tangshan.

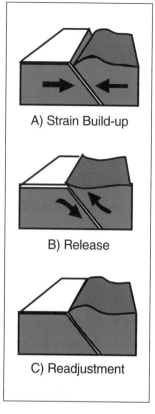

A) Strain Build-up

B) Release

C) Readjustment

The earth's plates move. The plate on the right has become stuck on the left plate (A). Eventually the strain releases (B) in an earthquake, causing a lot of shaking until the plates readjust (C).

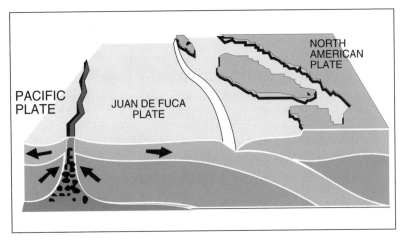

West of Vancouver Island, an oceanic ridge churns out new crustal material. As part of the Juan de Fuca Plate, the young crust slowly edges eastward, sliding under the North American Plate. Along the lower reaches, part of the plate melts and erupts as volcanoes.

In a serious west coast earth-quake, what we will we actually see, hear and feel? Will Richmond sweep out to sea on a tidal wave? Will the Lions Gate and Second Narrows bridges plunge into Burrard Inlet? Will the sea reclaim the hotels and government buildings ringing Victoria's Inner Harbour? The experts say not, but that doesn't mean we can afford to take earthquakes lightly.

Earthquakes unleash huge, ungovernable force on the terrain and the works of humanity. They warrant our respect and fear; they demand our best efforts to protect against their destructive ferocity. No one should underestimate their power to create devastation and outright terror.

Two main kinds of earthquake could strike coastal British Columbia, subduction and crustal earthquakes. A subduction earthquake has not occurred within recorded history, but we have experienced a major crustal earthquake within living memory; a 1946 quake killed one man and caused widespread damage on Vancouver Island. Older islanders remember all too well the results of a strong strike-slip or crustal earthquake in June 1946 with its focus northwest of Courtenay, probably near Mount Washington. In Campbell River, Port Alberni, Powell River, Courtenay and nearby Cumberland, plaster crumbled, walls gaped, windows shattered, chimneys and brick facings tumbled and crockery flew from kitchen cupboards. Waves ran up onto the shore and upset boats on Comox Lake and Georgia Strait, and one man drowned offshore at Deep Bay. Witnesses said Comox farm fields and the main street of Cumberland rippled in waves like shallow water over tideflats. The mid-island towns contained mostly wood-frame buildings which yielded and flexed with the shock, but there were hazardous exceptions.

Courtenay's elementary school, a two-storey wood and masonry building, suffered considerable damage inside and out. Chimneys plummeted down through the roof into the classrooms, and probably would have killed or injured many of the children inside. Fortunately the earthquake occurred on a Sunday morning when the school was empty. Moderate damage was widespread, and the shock broke windows in Victoria and frightened people as far away as Portland.

The Lower Mainland last felt a major earthquake in 1872. The epicentre was miles away, somewhere between the Fraser Valley and northern Washington State. Settlement in the area consisted mainly of Indians' and settlers' houses of flexible wood-frame or plank construction; little damage occurred and there was no reported loss of life.

We now have a general understanding of the kinds of earthquake that could affect this area, but we will never be able to calculate the exact outcome of any quake. Too many variables cloud the picture. Severity, duration and damage potential of The Big One are as unpredictable as its precise date. The only thing we can be certain of is that sooner or later, next week or a century from now, it will strike.

Today an earthquake of similar magnitude to 1872 or 1946 could cause severe damage in the Lower Mainland and on Vancouver Island, with heavy property loss and some loss of life. Population density in the area, plus our building methods and especially building sizes, make for a deadly combination. Heritage buildings and districts are among the areas at highest risk, since they were generally not built to our current earthquake-resistant standards. Tall and large buildings, buildings on soft landfill, and certain kinds of concrete structures also represent a hazard; all are plentiful here. Seismologists have predicted that a major earthquake in southwestern British Columbia, home of almost 10 ten per cent of Canada's population, would be the country's largest economic and social disaster caused by a force of nature.

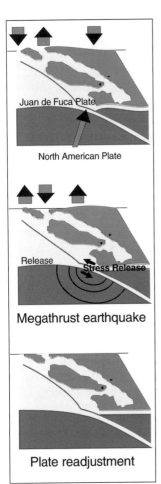

Juan de Fuca Plate

North American Plate

Release Stress Release

Megathrust earthquake

Plate readjustment

Megathrust earthquake cycle: When crustal plates collide along the Cascadia Subduction Zone off Canadas West Coast, a cycle of uplift and subsidence occurs as the earth's plates grind against each other. In the zones shown below, vertical movement of up to four millimetres a year has been recorded.

WHAT ARE WE WAITING FOR?

If we already know the potential danger, why are we quibbling about possible effects of The Big One? Why aren't we all living in totally earthquake-proof homes, spending our working and commuting hours in absolutely safe surroundings? Why aren't all our schoolchildren in buildings that can withstand a serious earthquake?

Money, as usual, plays a large part. Governments and taxpayers are reluctant to spend money on emergency plans for a disaster that may occur next week or not for another hundred years. Some have criticized British Columbia's government for economically and politically motivated inaction, for gambling that no major earthquake will occur during its term and that a later administration will bear the costs and the blame for widespread destruction. Until recently the province failed to take advantage of available federal matching grants, eagerly used by other provinces, allegedly because it was unwilling to contribute its share; new initiatives are correcting this situation. Earthquake preparation carries a large price tag. Immediate crises in plenty are exploding around us – environmental, health, social, cultural, economic, political – so why look further for possibly remote crises? Most significantly, perhaps, it's difficult for many people to imagine that an earthquake will really strike here.

Why should we concern ourselves personally with preparation? some people asked after the Loma Prieta quake in October 1989. Surely we pay taxes to deal with this kind of disaster, their argument

School buildings are especially vulnerable to earthquake damage because they may lack shear strength or lateral strength in large classroom areas. Many Mexico City schools collapsed in the September 1985 earthquake, fortunately before students arrived for morning classes.

ran, so if there's a serious earthquake the government should step in with aid.

A world of difference separates run-of-the-mill breakdowns from full-scale disaster, however. The city can send out crews to repair one broken water main or even half a dozen downed power lines. Major earthquake damage is another matter. Repairs can take days or weeks. No city or municipality can mobilize thousands of crews at once to repair a wrecked infrastructure of water, power, gas, sewer, transportation, communication and other services, and also assist individual homeowners. There aren't enough skilled people and necessary equipment – even with trained volunteers and emergency reinforcement from the private sector and neighbouring states and provinces – to scratch the surface. The cost of maintaining enough earthmoving equipment and operators to handle a major disaster, for example, would be astronomical. The people who are trained and committed may not be available when needed. They may be injured, absent, or prevented from reporting for duty by damaged roads and bridges. And their energies will be divided or even fully occupied by looking after their own families.

"You're on your own for 72 hours" is the standard government advice to citizens. It's the plain truth. Houses may burn;

Soil liquefaction can cause slumping or landslides, leading to severe structural damage. The March 1964 Alaska earthquake destroyed at least 75 houses in the Turnagain Heights subdivision of Anchorage. Slope failure began a minute and a half to two minutes after the start of the quake, which lasted for more than seven minutes in some areas.

some may even be torched or dynamited to protect essential service centres. Injured and dead people may go unattended for hours and perhaps days. Families may be separated. Businesses may close, some temporarily and some permanently. No government can do much to prevent these things from happening, or to help you overcome them immediately. There's a great deal we can all do as individuals, however, to prevent the worst damage and lessen its harmful impact.

CHAPTER 2
ALL
SECURE

No totally quakeproof home exists, even in countries where people have been designing them for centuries, but you can certainly achieve an earthquake-resistant home.

Wood-frame houses and low-rise apartments under four stories have the best chance of weathering a big quake safely, the experts say. A standard one or two-storey house is probably the safest structure to be in during or after a shake. Taller apartments and office buildings of recent construction – the more recent the better, as our building codes are steadily upgraded for earthquake safety – are also relatively safe. Unreinforced masonry buildings (URMs) – which are numerous in older areas of Victoria, Vancouver, New Westminster and Nanaimo – can be decidedly not safe. Reinforcement and other retrofits of URMs are so costly that many owners in California, where people are intensely earthquake-conscious, decide to demolish and rebuild rather than spend huge sums on trying to make beautiful but unsound heritage buildings earthquake-resistant.

An earthquake-resistant home will withstand a major earthquake relatively intact, protecting its fragile contents even if it suffers some damage. Naturally the most important possible contents are your family members, then your family pets, but the intactness of your home and possessions will add immeasurably to your comfort and wellbeing. In British Columbia we're fortunate in our economy, our construction methods and our social safety nets, compared to people in Armenia or El Salvador. Here, with a little preparation, you can reasonably expect to recover quickly from a great quake and get on with your life.

As owner, tenant, prospective buyer or builder, you won't have to think too deeply to find good reasons to make your home earthquake-resistant. Your home will be safer for you, your children and your visitors on a day-to-day basis if you take some of the precautions suggested in this chapter. Your home will weather other crises better; you'll reduce fire hazard by keeping flammable chemicals away from heat sources, for example, and you'll reduce potential gale damage by bracing tall chimneys.

Sometimes even an investigation takes care of the problem. I lay awake one summer worrying that an earthquake would topple a century-old chimney and send bricks crashing through my roof and ceiling like ceramic bombs. Then I realized that the ceiling of equally old fir planks, seasoned tough as steel, would stop any bricks cold. Earthquake precautions aren't always so easy, although many are almost as cheap.

A profit motive may also apply. We will sell our present house as "earthquake ready – bolted foundations, shatterproof safety film on windows, safety-latched cupboards, braced water tank . . ." and anything else that we get around to upgrading. Assuming that other people love techno-gadgets as much as I do, for the right price I may even allow myself to be parted from my custom gas valve wrench and freestanding spigoted water barrel, which cost a total of $19. Meanwhile, we'll be living as safely as possible.

You'll have to trust your hunches, ultimately, about how much preparation is enough, and how much is overdoing it. We decided our summer house on Vancouver Island wasn't worth heroic measures to protect against earthquake damage, even though it lies not far from a major fault and has dubious foundations of assorted stones, cedar posts and bricks. First, it's survived several big shakes since it was hurriedly built in 1889. Second, we decided that neither the house nor its material contents were unique, irreplaceable or particularly valuable. Earthquake precautions for that house consisted of storing a container of water in the cellar and not sleeping next to the window. Minimal preparation, true, but for that house it seemed an appropriate level of preparation. We'll have to wait to find out if it's the right choice.

A VIEW TO DIE FOR

Start making your home all secure by taking a close look around your setting. Consider an average family home, a one or two-storey wood-frame building on a municipally serviced lot. It sounds safe, yet depending on your location you could be vulnerable not only to an earthquake's primary effect of earth movement, but to secondary effects such as landslides and flooding. The good news is that British Columbians, unlike Californians, don't need to worry unduly about surface fissures. Even most of our crustal quakes occur at a moderately deep 20 to 30 kilometres below the surface and produce relatively little surface deformation. Several of our faults that seismologists believe extend "right

Salvaging a scant few personal possessions from the rubble of their homes, many residents of San Fransisco's hard-hit Marina District were left homeless after the October 1989 quake.

down to the basement" lie offshore either in Georgia Straight or off the west coast of Vancouver Island.

If you live in a potentially hazardous location, don't panic. Do plan some ways to reduce the hazard. You can upgrade your home for earthquake safety in a number of ways ̦ but you'll probably never quite get around to it if you don't assess your location first.

One hazard calls for special mention. Liquefaction occurs when loose soil gets wet and acts like a liquid under severe shaking. Artificial landfill and naturally occurring alluvial soils – such as sand dunes, beach sand or sandy soils found near river deltas – are most prone to liquefaction. In an earthquake, liquefaction undermines not only buildings but also roads, gas lines, sewers and water lines. Damage can be severe. In San Francisco's Marina District, which suffered heavy damage in the 1989 Loma Prieta quake, an estimated 73 per cent of the damage occurred on landfill. Ground movement of soft alluvial soil in Mexico City damaged more than 7,000 buildings and killed 10,000 people in the 1985 quake.

One glance at a map reveals why liquefaction is a concern in coastal British Columbia. Fraser Valley silts and artificial landfill are widespread throughout the Greater Vancouver Regional District, and in much of the area the water table is also high. Even the our international airport is built on alluvial Sea Island, scarcely above sea level. Victoria's Inner Harbour and parts of James Bay were dredged and reclaimed at the turn of century; the sub-cellars of major buildings in the area are said to ebb and flow with salt water at every change of tide.

Fortunately, there are big differences between this region and California or Mexico City. Mexico City grew from a village on a former lake bed, and is underlain by more than 40 metres of mud. The Marina District of San Francisco was once a lagoon, filled with sand to house the 1915 Panama-Pacific International Exposition. Neither site was extensively compacted or tamped, and until recently most buildings were not constructed on deep pilings. Most development in landfill or alluvial areas of coastal British Columbia is relatively recent, and relatively small scale. Multi-storey buildings are a post-war phenomenon in Richmond, for example, and building codes require the most recent to rest on deep pilings and well-compacted sites. One or two-storey houses will ride out even serious earthquakes with minor damage even on landfill. Liquefaction is certainly a concern in British Columbia, but not the deadly threat it can be elsewhere.

SAFETY IS NOT SKIN DEEP

Once you've checked out your location, consider the house's age and construction. Age isn't always apparent at a glance. Some old-timers are so thoroughly renovated that they may appear almost new, but make sure the renovation isn't merely cosmetic. Foundations are a particular concern in older houses, and they are usually expensive to upgrade or replace. Also consider the construction materials. A venerable brick or stone house may have incomparable charm, but if it's unreinforced it can sustain serious damage.

In California, after Loma Prieta and other recent quakes, some houses which survived the shaking in perfect condition structurally were knocked a metre or more off their foundations. The cost of getting them back in place was extremely high. A few hundred dollars spent on reinforcement beforehand could have saved tens of thousands of dollars later. The Loma Prieta quake alone damaged more than 23,000 homes, and most of the damage was from inadequate foundation anchor bolts, weak cripple walls or other foundation failure. Houses on concrete slab foundations, by comparison, usually fare well during earthquakes.

Bolting a house to its foundations during building adds almost nothing to the cost or time of construction. As a retrofit

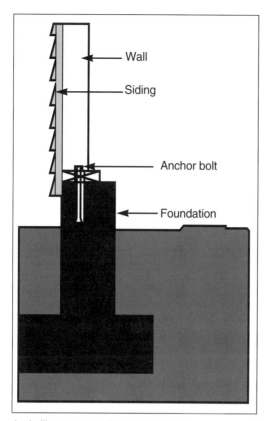

Installing an anchor bolt can help prevent your house from sliding off its foundations during a quake.

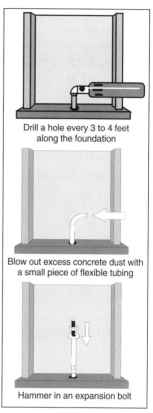

Drill a hole every 3 to 4 feet along the foundation

Blow out excess concrete dust with a small piece of flexible tubing

Hammer in an expansion bolt

Expansion bolts, available from your local hardware store, can strengthen your house during an earth-quake.

procedure, once the house is built, it's still not prohibitively expensive. Any reasonably handy homeowner can do this job. I have installed similar anchors myself without difficulty to frame in a small basement office; since everything was easy to reach, the whole process took less than an hour. On the other hand, I would cheerfully pay any amount to avoid working prone in a dark crawl space among wolf spiders the size of hamsters. We fretted for months about the expense of carrying out this grubby task in our present house, only to discov-

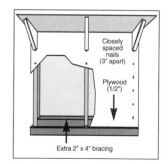

Closely spaced nails (3" apart)

Plywood (1/2")

Extra 2" x 4" bracing

Place plywood over a reinforced cripple wall and nail it to the studs for greater quake protection.

er that the diligent previous owner had already done the job. Before you invest in a gross of nuts and bolts, look to see if you're already firmly anchored. Check local building codes for requirements or guidelines on the size and spacing of bolts.

If you're installing your own anchor bolts, you'll need a power drill and half-inch concrete drill bit to drill down through the wooden horizontal sill plate of your house's frame into the top of the concrete foundation wall. If the sill plate is relatively accessible, you'll be able to use a standard drill or rotary hammer. If you have only a short crawl space, you'll have to rent or borrow a right-angle drill. Ideally you should drill every three or four feet, perhaps between every second vertical stud; the size and weight of your house, accessibility of the sill plate and foundation, and construction method, may require a different spacing. The ends of the sill plates are especially important, and it's worth your while to temporarily remove the wall covering or bracing to permit drilling.

Drill each hole to take a five and a half inch expansion bolt. The hole can be deeper than the bolt is long, but the diameter should be a snug fit. As you work, use a length of flexible tubing to blow concrete dust out of the hole. Caulk the hole, hammer in the expansion bolt, and screw on a washer and bolt as tightly as possible. Time consuming, possibly dusty, but easy – in theory.

In practice, some older or owner-built houses, or those with unusual design or location, may present complications. Floor joists may sit directly on the sill plate, for example, which means anchoring the house to the side and not the top of the foundation. You can tie sill plates to foundations by means of additional wood blocking and metal plates. If this seems too difficult, consult a building contractor.

California's Bay Area Regional Earthquake Preparedness Project (BAREPP) estimates the cost of having a contractor drive anchor bolts into foundations as $12 to $18 per foot of foundation (in 1990 U.S. dollars). Using these figures, you could expect to pay at most $3000 to upgrade a house with a 1200 square foot main floor. BAREPP estimates the cost of anchoring the house to the sill plate at $23 (1990 U.S. dollars) per foot of foundation. It's probably a bargain at twice the price for anyone who's not handy with power tools.

Older wood frame houses may present another weakness which can allow the house to slide off its foundations in an earthquake. A cripple wall or pony wall is a short wall which provides a crawl space between the foundation and the first floor; many

Some heritage homes and buildings are inadequately attached to their foundations. Owners often carry out beautiful restoration work but neglect to upgrade the structural elements. This Los Gatos house sustained serious damage when it shifted off its foundations in the October 1989 Loma Prieta quake.

are inadequately braced to support even a small house during an earthquake. Brace them from inside the crawl space by installing sheets of half-inch plywood nailed to the studs every three inches. Make sure there are at least two ventilation holes in each inter-stud section of plywood. If the sill plate is wider than the studs, you'll also need to nail in a two-by-four block top and bottom between each stud to have something to nail the plywood to. You can also strengthen a cripple wall from outside, but you'll have to remove and later replace any siding or exterior finishing such as stucco. BAREPP estimates this job at $15 to $20 (1990 U.S. dollars) per foot of foundation.

"Non-continuous foundation" usually spells out trouble and expense. Older buildings especially may rest on unconnected footings or piers which offer almost no support during an earthquake. At the very least the footings must be braced or tied together, and it may be wiser to think in terms of adding a new continuous concrete foundation. This will not be cheap.

A mobile home foundation may also need upgrading to prevent even a moderate quake from knocking the coach off its supports, a common cause of damage. One solution is to leave the wheels in place to limit the fall. Otherwise, the home should

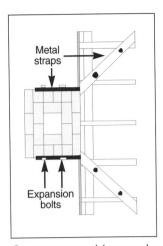

Brace your chimney to lessen the chance of it falling through your roof during a quake.

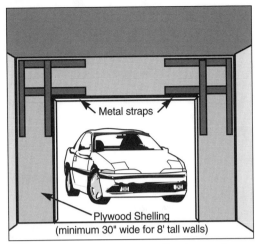

Metal straps

Plywood Shelling
(minimum 30" wide for 8' tall walls)

Bracing garage openings with plywood.

be bolted down and the foundations may also need reinforcement. Unless both sides of a double-wide mobile home are firmly tied together, a quake can shake them apart. Awnings must also be securely attached and strongly supported.

Some houses are built with a "soft storey" ground floor, often used as parking space, that can't support their weight. Many of the houses and apartments that collapsed in San Francisco's Marina District in 1989 failed for this reason. Owners had removed posts or walls in former basements to convert them to parking spaces, yet they still expected the weakened framework to support the weight of two or three storeys. Fifteen seconds of shaking destroyed the parking levels so thoroughly that some buildings were left with the former second storey leaning drunkenly on the sidewalk. One young woman was combing her hair in a second-storey bathroom when the earthquake struck; the next thing she remembered was a man reaching through the shattered window – at ground level –

Many San Fransisco houses and apartment blocks feature ground floor parking, sometimes a dangerous convenience. In some buildings, this created a "soft storey" inadequately braced against sudden ground movements. They collapsed during the October 1989 quake.

to take her arm and guide her out of the collapsed building.

Buildings that suffered such extreme damage had to be demolished. Many owners or tenants were denied permission to re-enter their homes because of the danger of further collapse, and had the dismal experience of seeing all of their possessions bulldozed along with their homes.

Rooms built over garages can present the same problem on a smaller scale. The walls may not be strong enough to support a second storey, and a typically large garage door provides no bracing whatsoever. A partial solution is to nail plywood above and on either side of the garage door opening. This provides shear strength, which prevents an earthquake from knocking your house sideways like an overloaded card table. There must be at least 30 inches of free space on either side for this plywood bracing to be effective. Otherwise, a contractor can add a steel frame around the door opening or add a new wall next to the garage as an external support.

Your house may also have decorative brick or stone facing. Unless it's anchored to the wall, it's almost guaranteed to part company from your house during an earthquake. You can certainly remove it and anchor it, but you'll have to decide whether it's worth the effort. Unless its location represents a special haz-

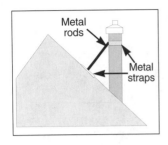

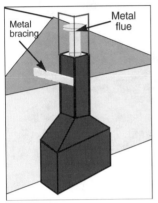

Brace your chimney and replace stone or brick chimney tops with metal flues.

ard, for example above shoulder height, you may want to wait for an earthquake to take care of the removal. Then, if you decide to replace it, attach it securely by fixing metal anchors between the masonry pieces as you glue or mortar the facing back in place.

DANGER BY DESIGN

Unusual structures also demand special attention. California publications warn prospective buyers about houses on stilts, houses with huge expanses of glass or many doors, houses with large overhangs, and houses with many split levels and complex geometry. This might sound as though a house with any design appeal is an earthquake trap, but it needn't be so. Many are adequately braced. Consult an engineer to see if reinforcement is required if you live in, or are considering buying or building, a house of this description.

Look upward for the next category of potential structural hazard. Roofs are usually a concern only if they're of heavy materials such as slate or pottery tiles. If the roof is extremely heavy, even if tiles stay in place, it can also intensify the house's earthquake-generated motion and cause serious damage to the entire building.

Unreinforced chimneys often topple in earthquakes, and can send a deadly shower of bricks or stone through the roof and ceiling. In the Loma Prieta earthquake, many chimneys were reduced to unidentifiable piles of masonry rubble. Chimneys that stand unbraced a metre or more above the roof, or against an outside wall, may be at risk. You may need to have someone dismantle the chimney above the roof and reconstruct it with reinforcement mortared right into the structure, or replace it with a metal pipe and flue. Check your local building regulations for the proper height and type in either case. A chimney standing against an outside wall will need metal straps to tie it firmly to the house. These are not jobs for the unqualified. Unless you really know what you're doing, hire a masonry contractor or fireplace specialist.

Hedge your bets by adding interior protection, too. The standard advice is to lay plywood sheets across your rafters in the attic, but no one bothers to suggest how to get plywood sheets through the average attic trapdoor without lifting the roof! It's easy enough if the house is still under construction, of course. Otherwise, use planks (they'll fit through the trapdoor) in a generous area around the chimney. Screw them to joists instead of nailing them to avoid knocking plaster into the rooms below. You won't need kiln-dried smooth-both-sides lumber; inexpensive rough spruce is featured regularly in lumber suppliers' seasonal sales.

Other elements can collapse in a quake if they're rickety, rotten or not firmly attached: large porches or balconies, outside stairs, garages and carports, and large unreinforced glass areas.

Trees near the house can also drop in uninvited during an earthquake. Look especially for substantial trees taller than the house, and "school-marms" or "widow-makers" (trees with multiple standards, visible splits or shattered branches). Oak trees are notorious for dropping heavy branches, but other deciduous and evergreen species can also cause damage, especially if they're shallowly rooted or undercut. Judicious pruning can prevent a post-earthquake headache.

While you're inspecting your home for potential earthquake hazards, particularly if you're a recent or prospective purchaser, look for signs of renovation. If doors or windows have been cut in walls, or if walls have been opened out to make larger rooms, the structure may have been weakened. Check that additions are strongly attached. If something looks doubtful, make sure the previous owner applied for building permits and inspection.

Also look for wall cracks, skewed doors and windows that don't open and close smoothly, and tilting floors. Not only may the house have settled but it may still be settling now. Find out whether the house was built on landfill and, if so, whether fill was compacted and pilings underlie the house. This isn't a concern in most single-family homes, but signs of serious settling should raise questions about what's underneath.

Former Vancouver Island coal mining centres including Nanaimo, Wellington, Cumberland and Ladysmith have their

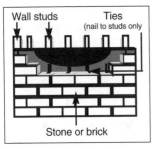

Tie brick or stone facing to the interior wall structure ot help prevent collapse in a quake.

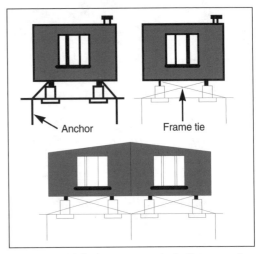

Bracing mobile homes can help them survive earthquakes without slipping off their piles.

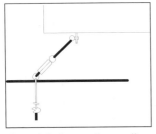

A mobile home frame tie.

own problems. Every few years a house sags into one of the many abandoned mine shafts which honeycomb parts of the island. Old workings are the most pernicious, since maps are often inaccurate. Check mine shaft and drift locations with your municipal planning or engineering department, especially if your house seems to be settling significantly. An earthquake is guaranteed to make it settle a lot faster and in unpleasant ways.

THE INSIDE STOREY

Shear strength could keep your house intact in an earthquake. The most effective way to add shear strength or lateral strength to a house wall is to nail plywood sheets to the inside surface of the wood studs; drywall can be installed right over the plywood. This is straightforward during construction, but in an existing home installing a shear wall means removing plaster or drywall, adding the plywood, then adding new drywall. Some older homes rely on bracing or diagonal blocking between wall studs for shear strength; this is inadequate. Not every wall needs the reinforcement, but a long wall not intersected by other bearing walls is a natural candidate. Materials for a shear wall are not overly expensive in themselves, but it can be a considerable pain in the pocketbook to tear out and replace existing walls. The natural time to retrofit is when you're planning a renovation. Don't leave this task for an earthquake to start; it may remove your drywall, but it could take the rest of the wall with it and possibly the roof. You'll do a neater and cheaper job.

Windows have little resistance to shear force. Enough motion sideways or in any other direction will shatter them, creating a flying glass hazard for anyone nearby. Large windows or window walls with little bracing are especially vulnerable. If you've ever broken a window or a glass tumbler you know how far glass travels when it shatters. Even crouching under a table or desk won't totally protect you from glass lacerations.

Tempered glass or wired glass will reduce the likelihood and extent of shattering, but either choice means replacing the glass in every window you treat. The price tag to replace every window in an average home would be thousands of dollars. You may choose to install wired glass or strong plastic panes ("bulletproof glass" is a common misnomer) in a few key locations where there's also a security risk, for example a window in or beside a door where a burglar could force entry. Tempered glass is not effective for security, the police advise homeowners, since experienced housebreakers have ways of smashing it anyway.

Security window film, fortunately, provides a cheaper and easier solution. Installed on the inside of windows it won't prevent shattering, but will hold shattered glass in place. This has several advantages. Most important, it reduces the risk of injury from flying glass during an earthquake. It also provides a minimal window covering afterward. If an earthquake has shattered your picture windows, you'll have better things to do than tour building suppliers in search of polyethylene film to tack over your empty window frames. Such materials (along with batteries, kerosene, candles and other emergency supplies) will quickly sell out anyway. Yet you'll need something to cover window openings to prevent rain or snow damage until you can get repairs, perhaps weeks later. Window film won't protect your home well against heat loss, and you'll have to replace it when you replace broken glass, but it's a good temporary measure. Police also reommend it to discourage break-and-entry; it won't keep out a

Even a moderate earthquake such as the June 1946 Vancouver Island quake can seriously damage foundations, or shift houses off their foundations. Foundation damage is often costly to repair.

thief who's determined to get in, but it may create enough of an impediment to send him off in search of easier pickings.

Window film is available in several thicknesses, and in tinted, reflective and scratch-resistant types. It generally allows only one per cent transmission of ultraviolet rays, and 80 to 85 per cent transmission of visible light. Clear film is invisible from either side of the window, and tinted film can reduce heat gain by 40 per cent. You can install it yourself at an approximate 1991 cost of two dollars per square foot, or have it professionally installed for about twice that amount. Suppliers will guarantee it for several years if it's professionally installed.

Two to four dollars a square foot can add up quickly to several hundred dollars or more for an average home. You may want to flag different windows for different treatments: wired glass for windows that could attract housebreakers, window film in children's rooms and frequently used living areas, no treatment for small out-of-the way windows.

All of these structural safety recommendations will guide you in upgrading or retrofitting your present home. Store them for future reference, too, in case someday you're building or buying a new house.

CHAPTER 3
WORLDLY GOODS

In 20 seconds an earthquake can redecorate your living quarters so thoroughly that you're still clearing away the mess several weeks later. Even if your home remains structurally intact its contents will be hurled around. Furniture, appliances, office equipment, kitchen utensils, groceries, toys, plants and ornaments all become missiles in the original sense of the word; they are sent aloft. This is hard to imagine if you haven't lived through it.

A television advertisement for a New Zealand insurance company makes a graphic argument for prevention over cure, and for insurance. If a picture's worth 1,000 words, this sequence is worth 100,000. Bookcases and cabinets crash full-length. Books and porcelain fall in broken heaps. Television and stereo equipment shatters on the floor. Ornaments fly and explode like grenades. A beautiful old grandfather clock smashes to kindling. Bottled preserves and other foods slather a sticky mess over the entire scene. And that's just the start. The ad lasts half a minute at most, perhaps a little longer than an average medium-large quake. The destruction is indescribable, heartbreaking, too dismaying to even consider cleaning up. If this were my home I'd want to drop a match in the mess and walk away. But most if not all of the damage shown in the New Zealand ad was preventable.

People who have cleaned up their homes after a disaster – tornado, flood, gale, break-in, fire – have some sense of what to expect in the way of earthquake damage. Tornados, floods and gales are at least somewhat predictable in some weather conditions. You may have enough warning to hide in the cellar before a twister or get valuables up off the ground before a flood. Earthquakes cheat. Emanating from kilometres underground, they're unaffected by season, weather, temperature or wind velocity. Happily, there's much we can do to prevent the worst earthquake loss.

SPONTANEOUS CONFUSION

Flammable or hazardous materials including painting supplies and cleaning fluids should be stored away from heat sources, close to the ground, and – in the case of potentially deadly combinations like ammonia and chlorine – away from each other. Consider the result if a bottle of solvent spills in an earthquake, for example, and at the same time electrical wires are torn from a damaged wall. The fumes quietly build to the point of spontaneous combustion. Then you come home, turn on the light switch, and a spark ignites into a flash fire.

Your chemicals may be stored in non-breakable plastic containers, but try upending one or two carefully in a sink. You'll find that some leak at the lid no matter how tightly they're sealed. Even the best, if they're hurled across the garage and impaled on your garden rake, won't stay leakproof long. Among the worst, yet most common, places for dangerous materials and chemicals are garages, basements, and other poorly ventilated areas. The best possible place for them is outside the house entirely, ideally in a locked and well ventilated garden shed.

If you've heard any earthquake preparedness advice at all, it's probably to secure your hot water tank. This is one of the most important things you can do, for two compelling reasons. First, a full hot water tank is extremely heavy, probably weighing in at around 150 kilograms. If it topples and bursts you'll instantly have 100 to 200 litres of scalding water on the floor. The electrical or gas connection will be broken, causing a serious hazard of explosion, fire or gas poisoning. Carpets or other floor coverings will be soaked, perhaps ruined. Anyone nearby could be injured or killed. Second, you'll need that water after the quake. If water services aren't restored within a few days, you'll quickly use the contents of your ice-cube tray, toilet tank (this is clean water, unlike the water in the toilet bowl) and possibly any water you've stored. If roads are impassable and tanker trucks can't deliver emergency water, you're in trouble. Your hot water tank will meet most of your water needs for days.

Strapping a water tank should take even a klutz no more than an hour and cost less than $10. When we tried it, however, the stud locator found the hot water pipe instead of the wall stud, and we confidently nailed a wooden brace into the only copper pipe in a three-metre expanse of wall. Scalding water sprayed out over all our coats, outdoor shoes and packsacks. It ran down the garage stairs to soak the dry cat food, which swelled to obscene proportions. The cats fled into the woods. The baby cried. And so

WORLDLY GOODS

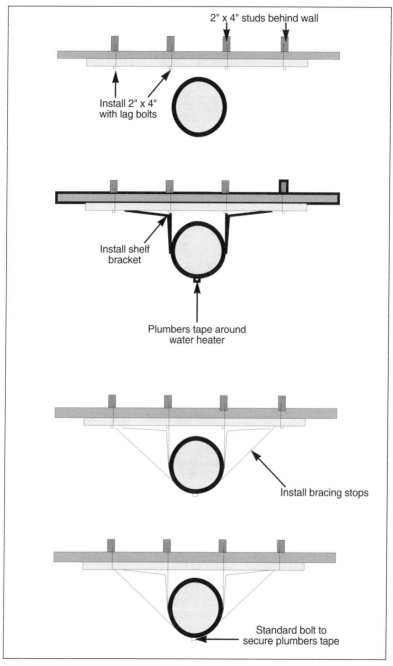

2" x 4" studs behind wall

Install 2" x 4"
with lag bolts

Install shelf
bracket

Plumbers tape around
water heater

Install bracing stops

Standard bolt to
secure plumbers tape

Water heater strapping installation.

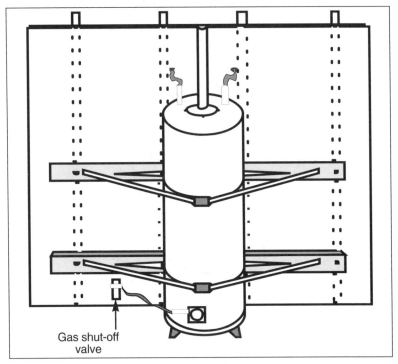

Strapping your hot water heater to the wall is an important safety measure you can do yourself.

Gas shut-off valve

on. The repair cost us $187, and that didn't include strapping the water tank. In fact, we were too humiliated to even think of asking the plumber to do this for us at any price. Most people find strapping the water tank cheap and easy.

To do the job right, you'll need a package of perforated metal plumber's tape, a few wood screws, and possibly a few scraps of wood. Wrap the plumber's tape right around the tank at top and bottom, and screw the ends tightly to the wall studs if the tank is close to a wall. If it stands out from the wall, first screw a suitable wood scrap into the wall studs to narrow the gap, and screw the plumber's tape to the wood. Once you've secured the hot water tank you can also prevent breaking of the gas line by having a gas fitter install a flexible hose or a loop of pipe between the tank and the gas line. Never use a flexible connector unless the tank is already strongly strapped in place – otherwise the tank could topple. Automatic shut-off valves which turn off the gas service at a certain level of vibration are also available from a commercial supplier for a few hundred dollars.

They can be useful for mobility impaired homeowners who can't turn off the valve if they smell gas, or for non-residential buildings where it won't cause serious problems not to have gas service for a few days after a quake.

Your furnace is probably bolted down – if not, this is another relatively quick job. An earthquake can send a furnace slamming across the floor and break gas, oil or electrical connections. A few expansion bolts now can save you the expense of a new furnace.

Heavy appliances can also skitter across a room with alarming agility during a quake. Tall ones, such as large refrigerators or upright freezers, can also topple full length. Lock the rollers on any appliances that have them, or if you don't really need the mobility, remove the rollers altogether. You can also restrain most appliances by connecting them to a stud in the wall behind them with a metal strap.

LATCH IT OR LOSE IT

Cupboards in your kitchen, bathroom and other areas hold more things than you'd like to think possible. Next time you're spring cleaning, try emptying all the kitchen cupboards at once. Chances are you'll soon have foods, crockery, utensils and the rest of the miscellany stacked up on every available surface. Now imagine all that on the floor, most of it broken or spilled, and the task of cleaning it up. Usually the very thought is enough to send you to the hardware store for cupboard latches. Waste no time before installing them on kitchen, bathroom, or laundry room cabinets. Save enough for your china cabinet. If your best plates end up as crockery fill in the bottom of flower pots, it's insult added to injury.

Several types of latch will effectively keep your cupboards closed during an earthquake. If you're willing to mount them on the outside of the cabinet, you have more choices. A simple hook and eye will do the job, as will a thumb-turn latch. Some attractive ones are available in brass and other finishes. If aesthetics or design requires an interior mounting, you're restricted mainly to magnetic or mechanical "push latch" types, or child-proof latches. Remember, with these in place, every time you open the cupboard you'll have to take an extra second to open it a few centimetres and reach in to release the latch. These may be the most secure interior-mounting latches, however, and the extra opening action soon becomes second nature.

Some cupboards defy any interior mounting because of a large overhang or tight fit with other cupboard doors. This may

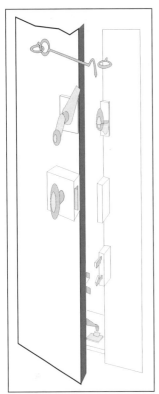

When selecting latches, consider looks and ease of use.

force you to choose between marring the outside of the cupboard with an exterior latch and reserving that cupboard for unbreakable, unspillable items.

Most furniture doesn't create a hazard during an earthquake, but there are exceptions. Wall systems, tall bookcases, china cabinets, wardrobes, Welsh dressers, armoires or other tall pieces will almost certainly crash to the floor during a major quake. Not only will they destroy much of their contents, but they can injure anyone nearby and block your avenue of escape.

Consider a worst-case scenario: your wall system full of television and stereo equipment falls on you during a shake, breaking your leg and causing glass lacerations. You struggle out eventually, but you smell gas and see smoke. Your children are trapped upstairs in their bedrooms. Will you have time to rescue the children and get out the door before fire engulfs your home? It's not a question you should ever have to answer. Prepare accordingly.

You may be wise to move some pieces immediately. A tall bookcase next to a bed or a heavy wardrobe beside a room's only door can create real problems. If you're using a wall system as a freestanding room divider, move it against a wall where you can anchor it and instead divide the space with a low bookcase or chest, or a lightweight folding screen.

Affix tall pieces of furniture to the wall with angle brackets at the top and sides, screwed into wall studs, or tie the pieces to the wall with metal straps as you would a refrigerator. If the angle brackets would create an ugly blot on your decor, take a slightly different approach. Install a long screw through the back of the piece, inside a length of plastic tubing between the piece and the wall, and into a wall stud. Use a washer to prevent the screw head from pulling free. This will only work if the back panel is strong enough to withstand some force; a flimsy fibreboard veneer won't hold the cabinet's weight. If you're really concerned about appearance, camouflage the screw head, washer and plastic tube with paint or wallpaper. Many china cabinets, wall systems and desks consist of a base unit with a hutch resting on it; in addition to fastening both sections to the wall, tie them firmly together with a metal bracket at the back. Otherwise your china hutch can walk off its base during an earthquake, taking some of your most fragile possessions with it. Filing cabinets also need to be strapped to a wall because of their weight and frequent top-heaviness.

A collection of plates leaning on a narrow shelf around a room can change in seconds from a homey decorating feature to a mess you'll have to sweep up. If you attach the plates to the wall with velcro fasteners, they'll stay in place through considerable shaking.

Bookcases may need further attention even if they're properly anchored. Books are heavy; the contents of a bookcase spilling over your head may not prove fatal, but the experience is guaranteed to leave you bruised, surly and picking up broken-backed books for hours. A dowel guardrail in front of the books on every shelf will prevent them from sliding off. If appearance doesn't matter, it will be quicker and cheaper to use the plastic-coated wire sold for hanging cafe curtains. Usually this attaches at the sides

Potential hazards.

with small closed-eye screws. And nothing dictates that your books must be upright on their shelves. Try leaning them at an angle as some bookstores and libraries do. You can still read the spine text and lift them out easily. In bookcases or other tall cabinets, make sure that adjustable shelves can't slide out of their frame. Shelves resting on four pins or supports, without any indentation or attachment, need further restraint.

Other items on tall shelves may need relocating. A standard guideline is to remove any heavy or breakable objects from shelves higher than the head of your shortest family member. Place pottery, metal or glass ornaments on lower shelves or on the floor unless you can anchor them securely.

OFF THE WALL IDEAS

Wall-hung mirrors and pictures can fall to the floor, spraying glass shards. Use angle brackets or various kinds of specialized mirror clips to hold them firmly to the wall. If a mirror is mainly a decorating feature and you can afford to lose some brightness in the reflection, you could coat it with safety window film. This is worth a try on pictures, too, but reduced clarity may spoil your enjoyment of the image. If your lifestyle features a mirrored ceiling and a waterbed, contemplate what will happen if the two meet forcibly in a quake. The outcome is guaranteed to deflate your ego and dampen your ardor. Do your stargazing outdoors; move your bed if it's near a window. Keep blinds and curtains drawn when you're asleep.

Hanging plants, light fixtures and mobiles can swing wildly, causing injury or damage, or crash to the floor. Try moving plants and mobiles to corners or other low-traffic areas where you're unlikely to find yourself wearing your philodendron. Anchor their hanging hooks securely into wood studs, not just into plaster or drywall, and close open hooks with tape, wire or a pinch of your pliers. Better still, replace your hanging plants with silk imitation plants in lightweight baskets and keep living plants on shelves or surfaces below waist height. At the very least, repot hanging plants in lightweight, unbreakable plastic or basketry containers.

Mobiles in a child's room, no matter how light they are, should never hang directly over the bed. A baby could get tangled in the cords, especially if earthquake shaking or damage prevents you from coming to her immediately, and even cardboard mobiles have sharp corners and crosspieces.

Lamps and light fixtures can part company from ceilings in a hurry during an earthquake unless they're firmly attached. Many are held in place only by their electrical wires; for the lightest, this is probably adequate. If the fixture or shade is glass, metal or ceramic, also anchor the fixture with a decorative chain or screw it to a ceiling joist, depending on the design. Fluorescent tube lighting is potentially the most dangerous, since the metal fixtures can pull free of their ceiling bolts and descend with a crash. Support chains or wires are also needed to prevent the kind of damage that occurred in a number of California schools in recent earthquakes. Ceiling fans are usually well attached, but check to be certain.

You don't need to protect your possessions against an earthquake, only those you want to keep. Electronic equipment, artworks, ornaments, memorabilia, computer equipment, musical instruments and other cherished personal belongings are grievous to lose and often costly to replace. Many items of sentimental value are irreplaceable at any price.

No single solution will protect all your possessions, but your first and best choice may be Velcro or another hook-and-loop tape fastener. Anchor equipment, art and ornaments to a hard surface with one or two Velcro strips, depending on the item's mass. Velcro comes in several weights; for a television set or computer you'll want heavy duty. The backing of any such fastening may leave a gummy residue or damage the surface; if you don't want to blemish your fine wood furniture, find another place for the equipment where you can secure it, or strap it to the wall behind. Light duty strips will adequately hold smaller, lighter objects in place. So will hold-fast putties, which usually peel off without leaving a residue. Other precious things may be better stored in drawers and brought out for special occasions.

This is the time to contemplate your real values and valuables. If you think about it, you may well conclude that your foremost treasures are memorabilia – family photos, the first valentine your child made for you, the decoration from your wedding cake, your grandfather's watch. When the building housing my office burned to the ground, I didn't give a second thought to my furniture and books worth a few hundred dollars. I mourned the radio my parents gave me on my twelfth birthday, never mind that it pulled in only one station. Market value: maybe five dollars. Intrinsic value: priceless and irreplaceable. After a tornado struck Edmonton in July 1987, people combed the wreckage of their Evergreen Trailer Park homes for days, desperate to find their family snapshots and keepsakes.

Mentally divide your personal effects into three categories: can't live without, rather like, and couldn't care less. Give away or sell the couldn't-care-less things. Forget the rather-like ones except to anchor them if they're likely to fly across a room at you. That leaves possessions the loss of which would impair your pleasure in life. Your decisions about what to do next with these treasures – put them in a safety deposit box, make copies for other relatives, keep them where they are and enjoy them – will depend on their size and function. You're not going to put your banjo in a safety deposit box or give a copy of your personal diaries to your teenaged nephew.

A MATTER OF POLICIES

Buy insurance if you have even the slightest aversion to living out of a plastic garbage bag in a grocery cart for the rest of your life.

Maybe you think your possessions aren't worth insuring. But how much can you afford to lose? This is really the operative question when you're making a decision about insurance. Perhaps you can replace your home and all of your possessions with the spare change from your next month's pay cheque; most people can't. True, you could pay insurance premiums year after year without getting a penny back but, if ever you need it, insurance can repay your premiums many times over. About $100 will add earthquake coverage to an average insurance policy; like flood and other disaster coverage, it's not usually included.

Some exceptions could make insurance not worth your while, however. Because of its non-continuous foundations our summer house on Vancouver Island would cost us about $1,000 per year for earthquake insurance alone. Our insurance agent advised us not to bother. The most likely damage would be loss of the brick chimney (not a total loss, I suppose, since we could always use the extra bricks to shore up the dubious foundations) and that would cost about $1,000 to repair. New foundations would cost a minimum of $5,000. We decided to pay for the repair once, when we needed it, rather than pay the same amount in premiums every year.

A word of caution about insuring specialized or collectors' items; make sure that you're insuring for their true value, preferably replacement value, and not for a generic amount. After a flood ruined many old and rare books, we found that our otherwise first-rate policy insured books at a flat rate suitable only to book-of-the-month selections. It took no account of collectors' books. We couldn't replace our books anyway, but we could have consoled ourselves better with fair recompense.

Books, artworks, jewellery, antiques, electronic equipment, classic cars and other specialized goods should be listed on their own floater policy which recognizes their true or intrinsic value. For cars, artworks and jewellery you'll probably have to pay for a professional appraisal every few years. If you own such things and value them, it's worth your while.

This doesn't mean you can afford to be nonchalant about the risk of theft, earthquake damage or any other loss. Police advise, in the context of residential theft, that insurance is not a solution. If your house is broken into repeatedly, eventually no insuring body will issue a policy. And of course insurance doesn't give you back the things you've lost, only an approximation.

A household inventory will help you make the most of your insurance if you ever need to make a claim for any reason. Insurance agents used to ask homeowners or tenants to list all property – with descriptions, purchase price and date, present value, and serial numbers – and keep the list somewhere safe outside the home, perhaps in a safety deposit box. Now you can buy booklets that step you through an average house, room by room, and even list some common items. Or you can buy a computer program to do all this and more on screen. In either system you just fill in the serial numbers, prices and other details. Any of these documents should adequately support an insurance claim if your possessions are fairly typical.

If you own anything exceptional or costly, or if you have any kind of floater policy, you need to go a step further to document your belongings. Go through your house room by room with a polaroid camera; stand in the middle of the room and take enough photos to record everything in it. Lay out the contents of jewellery boxes, silverware drawers, and closed cabinets. Better still, film them with a video camera, simultaneously recording your own audio description of the objects you're taping. If you don't own and can't borrow a camcorder, you should be able to rent one for a modest fee plus deposit. Update the record with a new videotape every year or whenever you make major purchases that warrant inclusion. Store the tape somewhere safe, preferably in a different location.

Looting of homes and businesses after an earthquake seems to be much less significant than popular mythology suggests. People tend to pull together after a disaster, spontaneously helping each other until things return to normal. Or maybe thieves are just too busy guarding their own treasures to pilfer yours.

Tenants, like homeowners, can improve their odds for surviving The Big One without serious loss or damage. Much depends on the building landlord's financial situation and personal philosophy. If you rent a house, part of a house or a suite in a small building, perhaps you can persuade the landlord to upgrade. Or perhaps you can negotiate a rent rollback if you pick up some costs. In a multi-unit building, it's certainly worth your while to learn the building's age and construction, and its safety features. Then lobby for any retrofits you think are necessary. Enlist your neighbours' support. A tenant committee will get a better hearing than an individual.

Meanwhile, make any improvements you can manage out of your own pocket. Installing window film, securing the hot water tank, anchoring hanging fixtures and adding cupboard latches are all relatively inexpensive and easy. And by all means insure your property for its full worth under the most complete policy you can find.

If your building is old (especially if it's unreinforced masonry) or you can't get even minimal co-operation from your landlord, you might as well avoid a forced emergency move without your prized possessions. Move to safer quarters now.

A wise word on worldly goods comes from Surviving the Big One, an informative and entertaining Los Angeles Fire Department videotape narrated by firefighter Henry Johnson. After touring his own house in search of earthquake hazards, Johnson advises that once you've taken every possible precaution, it's time to detach yourself emotionally from your home and everything in it. Your belongings may be dear to you, but if ultimately you lose them, it's fruitless to carry a burden of grief for inanimate objects. Your life and your family's lives are infinitely more precious.

An old woman in the midwestern United States, left homeless a few years ago by a tornado, told Red Cross worker Lynn Orstad something she would never forget: "Well, honey, I tell you. Tornado came but I'm still here, and I've got my quilt, and I don't cry over anything that's not going to cry over me."

"I just loved her," Orstad said. "She was a woman of the world.

CHAPTER 4

ZERO DOWNTIME

Small businesses are particularly vulnerable to earthquakes, since many occupy rented or leased buildings that are not earthquake resistant, and have perishable or time-dated inventory. All too often they are also undercapitalized. After a moderate 1983 California quake, about one-quarter of the businesses in the affected area closed permanently. The October 1989 Loma Prieta quake, in 15 seconds of seismic shaking, damaged 3,547 businesses and destroyed 367.

Owners suffer bankruptcy and personal setbacks when businesses fail after a disaster. Employees are thrown onto the breadlines. Customers must find new suppliers of products or services. But the impact goes far beyond personal loss.

Small businesses form the economic backbone of any community. They generate a major portion of the tax base which in turn paves roads, underwrites social assistance and unemployment cheques, runs schools and hospitals, attracts tourism, and pays other workers' salaries. After Santa Cruz's Pacific Garden Mall, a picturesque "old town" shopping district, was the scene of three deaths and heavy damage in October 1989, the shockwaves of business closures and bankruptcies soon spread far beyond the zone of physical destruction. Business survival after a major earthquake ensures not only personal economic survival but also community survival.

"If people stop and think about it, the economic disaster which follows immediately afterwards sometimes can be enough to throw a smaller town completely out – it can give quite a hardship," says Lynn Orstad of the Canadian Red Cross.

All businesses of any size need to consult insurance agents, engineers, and suppliers of utilities and other services in order to develop suitable emergency plans. Large businesses, including governments, need their own site-specific emergency plans and procedures. This book cannot replace consulting services; it can only offer general information and draw your attention to problem areas.

Potential dangers for small businesses include injury to staff or customers, and physical damage to the building, equipment or

Poor masonry construction methods caused failure of part of the Pallante factory in Campania, Italy in a November 1980 earthquake. Unreinforced masonry buildings—mainly brick, stone or adobe—are particularly susceptible to earthquake damage.

inventory. In these two areas, perhaps with greater complexity, business hazard is similar to residential hazard. A third area presents special difficulties for businesses in addition to whatever personal difficulties face employer or staff: a business lucky enough to come through a big quake relatively unscathed by injury or physical destruction will still almost certainly suffer some interruption of business. The key to business survival is to keep the interruption to hours or days, rather than weeks or months. The bogeyman of business is time lost to trade, or downtime.

On a personal level, most of us can't afford to lose much work time, whether we work for someone else or for ourselves. Unless you're a salaried employee of government or a major corporation, your income is probably not protected against time lost because of earthquake damage.

A couple of months' unplanned lost work can mean missed mortgage and car payments, and a rapid erosion of the savings account. Ask yourself: How much work can I afford to lose? Sit down with a pencil and your household accounts or last year's income tax forms, and work it out. The answer will probably unnerve you, and convince you to thoroughly protect yourself from earthquake income loss.

An earthquake that temporarily closes your business won't necessarily affect your competitors. Any business better positioned to move into the post-earthquake market can easily take your market share, and keep it long after you re-open. It's earthquake mythology to think otherwise, says Dr. Charles Thiel, a Stanford University consulting engineer and earthquake researcher. Many business people accustomed to working in changing environments believe they can improvise a recovery from earthquake damage. Thiel says, "In the emergency management business there is one fundamental truth. You can do nothing in the emergency period that you have not thought through at your leisure before the emergency." He also warns against thinking that we can do nothing to prepare. We can do plenty.

Avoiding injury must be the first priority for both those who normally spend their time in the workplace and for others who may happen to be there when a major quake strikes. People in the work force spend a third or more of their daily lives on the job, and there's a real possibility of an earthquake occurring while they're there. Most people work in circumstances where others make the decisions about safety and emergency planning. Employees or even local managers may not have the power to decide to reinforce a structure or write emergency response contracts. As a result, employees are often restricted to planning for their own safety in their working environment.

Employers should train staff members in earthquake response, provide written instructions and schedule regular full drills. Food, water, lighting and heating supplies should be kept in a safe storage area. There should be at least three days' supplies for a typical number of employees and visitors during working hours. Emergency repair tools and materials will also come in handy.

Home earthquake preparation is an essential part of business earthquake preparation. Employees are naturally concerned foremost about their families' safety; employers who expect otherwise are unrealistic, and in for a rude awakening. Henry Renteria, Oakland's director of emergency services, had to hastily reassign tasks to junior staff and staff from other departments after the Loma Prieta quake. He had expected senior staff to go home to check on their families, but then to return to work to handle the crisis. Instead, they stayed at home, placing a greater burden on already stressed co-workers.

The solution, emergency planning co-ordinators believe, is to have employees thoroughly prepare their homes and families. After an earthquake they'll know where family members are and have confidence in their ability to respond properly. Richmond emergency planning co-ordinator Don MacIver goes one step further; essential emergency workers' families are checked out by co-workers in radio-equipped trucks, who relay status reports to the emergency operations centre. Employers should set clear procedural guidelines – employees may go home to check their families but return quickly, for example – and provide earthquake preparation information for employees to take home. Bulk purchase of supplies, made available free or at cost, would also assist families to prepare without having to shoulder extra expenses.

A BUSINESS HAZARD HUNT

Your workplace may contain some of the structural and non-structural hazards mentioned in earlier chapters. At one end of the scale, minor damage may cause no injuries and interrupt business only for a day or so. At the other extreme is total building collapse causing death or serious injury to occupants.

In the best of all possible worlds, we would spare no expense to make all business sites as earthquake-resistant as our present technology permits. In practicality, small businesses must set priorities and invest in as much hazard mitigation as they can afford. Areas where employees and customers tend to congregate and areas used in evacuation should get first attention. *Earthquake Preparedness: A Key to Small Business Survival* suggests ranking hazards this way:

1. *building collapse*
2. *obvious dangers for occupants and passersby*
3. *threats to occupants leaving the building*
4. *interruption of essential services*
5. *costly damage to the building and its contents*

Start by scouting around your office as you would your home, with special attention to structural hazards related to location and underlying soils, building foundations and soft storeys, unreinforced chimneys, add-ons such as porches and decks, weak walls and windows. Pay special attention to elevators. These should be fitted with seismic switches to prevent their use after a quake, or at least bear signs warning people not to use them after a quake. Stairways will be key exit routes; an engineer or contractor can advise you on making them flexible at landings or integrating then with walls and floors. Prevent debris from filling stairways by ensuring strong enclosure walls and strong attachments for lights, pipes and other utility fixtures. Signs, roof parapets, brickwork or awnings over entrances can cause serious injury if they part company from the building, as they did at hundreds of sites during the Loma Prieta quake. The sidewalk in front of a store or office building is considered its greatest danger spot. Falling debris at an entrance has killed many people who unwisely tried to flee the building.

Unreinforced masonry commercial buildings, like URM residential buildings, are at high risk. Some especially hazardous building types are common in business or industrial sites. In the 1985 Mexico City quake, concrete slab buildings and other concrete buildings of six to 10 storeys were particularly prone to collapse because of the vibration frequency of that quake; unfortunately, no one can predict at what wavelength a quake will resonate. Concrete "tilt-up" buildings can also fail. The term "tilt-up" refers to a construction method in which a concrete slab floor is poured on site, then used as a mould to pour each of the walls, which a crane lifts into upright position. In an earthquake, unless the connections are strongly reinforced, the roof and walls can simply shake apart and crash to the ground. Tall buildings may be structurally safer than mid-size buildings in a moderate earthquake, but are at greater non-structural risk. Because they sway with the quake's motion, equipment and furniture can be thrown about wildly. If you own or lease in a potentially hazardous building, and are uncertain of its construction or improvement history, call in a consulting engineer without delay. The building may need major reinforcement. If not, you and your employees will appreciate the reassurance.

Then look for potential non-structural hazards including hot water tank and other utilities, hazardous chemicals, tall cupboards and bookcases, hanging lamps and plants, electronic equipment and ornaments. Desks and chairs rarely overturn in earthquakes, but other furniture needs attention. Freestanding partitions will fall, especially if they support shelves of books or equipment. Avoid arranging them in long straight rows; create zig-zag patterns instead. Bolt them to the floor, desks or walls if possible. Anchor counters and display cases. Bolt tall filing cabinets to each other and to the wall. Brace or bolt together tall shelving units, or fasten them to the wall. Bolt valuable equipment to the floor. Replace glass containers with plastic wherever possible. Make sure that any equipment or merchandise you can't secure is relocated to prevent injury in crowded areas or blocking of evacuation routes. Security window film is also a

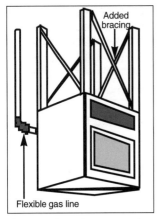

Space heaters can be dangerous if they fall from celings during a quake. They are easy to brace, for added quake safety.

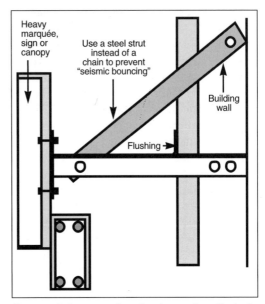

Secured signs on storefronts are less likely to collapse onto the sidewalk below during a quake.

good investment for windows and display cases.

Damage to contents – inventory and equipment in particular – may be greater than structural damage for small businesses. Retail stores may contain heavy cash register stands, and heavy overhead objects including large pipes and hanging space heaters. Stores usually display merchandise on shelves, racks or display islands. If an earthquake tosses goods from every rack, even light and non-breakable items such as children's stuffed toys, you can expect a good deal of picking up. Consider guard rails as in home bookcases to keep things more or less in place. Retailers who specialize in fragile and valuable merchandise such as antiques, fine housewares or artworks face a special challenge. Display pieces can be held in place unobtrusively by guylines of near-transparent fishing

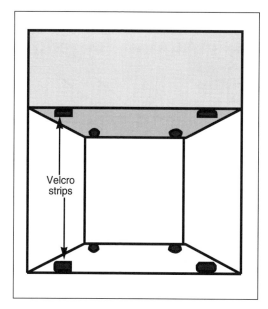

Velcro strips on the bottom of heavy office equipment can stop it from sliding off desks or tables during a quake.

Velcro strips

monofilament, or weighted with small sacks containing sand or shot. Unusually valuable pieces may warrant a special close-fitting plexiglas case. Make sure you also firmly anchor cabinets, pedestals or display cases to the floor or wall.

Office space may hold cabinets, emergency power generators, and computer and communications equipment which is both heavy and fragile. Manufacturing businesses may have heavy machinery. Bolt down, attach, move, reinforce or otherwise eliminate any hazards you identify. Most important, after your initial hazard hunt and improvements, remember to incorporate your changes into everyday business operations and future plans.

No small business, even a one-person enterprise, can afford to regard insurance as optional. It's a necessity. See the previous chapter for some good reasons; your insurance agent will be happy to tell you a dozen more. Replacement of damaged items is only one dimension of commercial earthquake insurance; another is liability. Although Canada is less litigation-prone than the United States, it's worth noting that many people there have been awarded substantial compensation for earthquake damage or injury sustained on business premises. If a falling display rack injures a customer or employee, or fire consumes a piece of jewellery left for repair, you may well be liable. Eliminating hazards is your first move, but follow it with a good insurance policy.

Computers can topple during earthquakes. They should be secured.

Don't forget to compile an inventory, ideally on film and in writing like a household inventory, to speed settlement.

An emergency response plan is the other absolutely essential element of earthquake preparedness. Any small business with more than a handful of employees needs the services of an emergency planning consultant. Very small businesses can draw up their own. In either case, the vital part of the plan is education, training, and drill.

Sometimes the only preparation possible is to train employees how to respond to an earthquake – including taking cover, and not rushing outside – and to post warning signs in elevators, entrances and other key locations warning against use after an earthquake.

PASSWORD: PARANOIA

Small businesses typically experience earthquake damage beyond the common or garden variety. Inventory, equipment and records are all vulnerable, warns *Earthquake Preparedness: A Key to Small Business Survival*. Perhaps at greatest risk are electronic equipment and records stored on electronic media, especially in computers.

Desktop, laptop and notebook personal computers are the mainstay of small business these days. Most use removable floppy disks as well as hard disk storage, which is notoriously volatile and susceptible to failure caused by power outages or minor jolts. The rule of thumb for desktop computers and similar equipment is that any object about twice as tall as it is wide may overturn; other objects may slide. Don't rely on the stopping power of those little rubber feet on the corners. True, they will prevent you from moving your computer without a hideous screech and black streaks across your desk. They'll do absolutely nothing to stop an earthquake from hurling your computer at the far wall where it will fall to the floor with a merry tinkle.

You can secure computers in several ways. You can add a lip or guardrail around the edge of your desk or computer station. You can attach each of the components to the desk with a sturdy leash. Or you can use heavy-duty Velcro or another loop fastener to fix the components to the work surface. A Key to Small Business Survival suggests using hook strips or pads on the bottom of the equipment, and loop strips or pads on the work surface. Make these twice as large as the hook patches so you don't need to place the equipment precisely, which can be difficult with heavy pieces. Test the adhesive bond after 24 hours and at intervals afterward.

If you like to roam around with your keyboard or find all this attaching too restrictive, weigh the relative costs and nuisance factors. A good monitor is fragile and will cost at least several hundred dollars to replace; a CPU will cost from a thousand to many thousands; a keyboard will cost only about $100 and may not break anyway because it's relatively light. If you use a mainframe computer instead of smaller personal computers, you'll need to put cabinets on castors to absorb the shock of ground motion, but tether them to the floor. This may call for special floor bracing and electrical supply protection, for which you'll need expert help.

Lost time is the real issue with damaged or destroyed business equipment. Even after a major quake you can probably replace computer hardware within a week or so. Data are another matter. There are people who work for months without backing up, and who have lost an entire day's work because they never got around to hitting the save keys. I back up religiously, myself, having seen too many files vanish into the twilight zone. I've always felt the only appropriate password for file backup was "paranoia." If you can afford to lose a week's work, back up

Chairs, desks and tables rarely overturn but counters and casework should still be anchored.

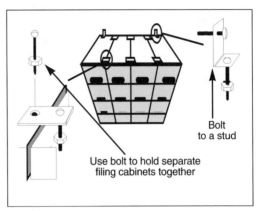

Bolt
to a stud

Use bolt to hold separate
filing cabinets together

Filing cabinets can topple during a strong quake. Securing them is easy

weekly. If you can only afford to lose a day's work, back up daily.

Even if you back up like clockwork, you may not be storing your backups safely. There's no point storing them in your office; an earthquake that destroys your computers or disks there will probably destroy your backups too. Instead, use a different earthquake-resistant location with good security such as your home, if it's well separated from your workplace, or the office of a trusted friend. Safety deposit boxes are risky for storing disks or tapes because metal can scramble electronically stored data. Don't put them in a fireproof safe, either, unless it's a specially-insulated ultra-high temperature safe designed for data storage.

Paper files are still the preferred means of keeping records for many small businesses. They are less vulnerable to power failures and ground motion associated with earthquakes, but are extremely vulnerable to the major post-earthquake hazard of fire. You need to protect against losing information in paper records as thoroughly as in electronic records. At the very least, make copies of your essential

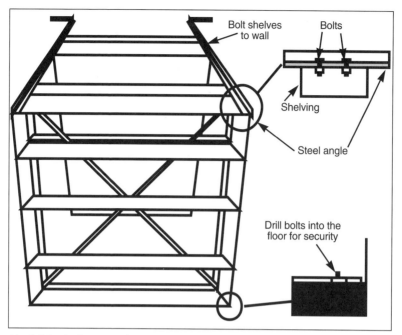

Unstable shelves can be solidified with a few bolts and extra steel.

papers including contracts, deeds, insurance policies, stocks and bonds, personal credit cards, business credit arrangements, accounts due and payable, and work in progress for clients. Some of these you may also want to physically store (if you don't already) in a first-rate fireproof safe, which should also be impact-resistant. Consider also storing in a safe any materials or papers borrowed from clients and, of course, any cash on hand.

A recent issue of *National Geographic* tells a poignant cautionary tale to accompany three extraordinary photographs showing San Francisco devastated by earthquake and fire in 1906. Edith Irvine, a young woman visiting the city, captured 60 images on glass negatives. She probably preserved her plates by hiding them from the authorities, who were confiscating photographers' work to prevent adverse publicity (similarly, the official death count was 498 out of 400,000, although one researcher now believes about 3,000 died).

"But in a sense, the terrible flames she recorded also consumed her career," Thomas Y. Canby writes of Irvine. "Records involving her father's ownership of several major mines were destroyed when fire ravaged City Hall. With the family fortune in legal limbo, the young photographer apparently could no longer afford to make pictures."

BUSINESS AS USUAL

Even with the best preparation, you'll spend hours after an earthquake sweeping up broken glass, picking up scattered files, safety-checking your building, calming staff and customers, and trying to get home to your family. Once you've handled the immediate crisis, you may still be unable to get back to normal because of power failure and disruptions to transportation and other services.

Sometimes business is urgent enough to carry on however and wherever. Carolyn Lloyd of Victoria, caught in San Francisco during the Loma Prieta quake, spotted a woman sitting on a parking lot curb in front of a beauty salon while the hairdresser neutralized her perm solution. The alternative if she'd waited was a bad chemical burn, or baldness. Whatever it takes, do get back to business as soon as possible, even if it means selling goods from a card table on the sidewalk.

Government – federal, provincial and in this case especially municipal – is also a business, and in smaller centres may be the largest business and employer in town. It's especially important for government to be back in operation at the first possible moment after an earthquake to handle not only disaster matters but also business as usual. San Francisco area local governments and the California state government are still slogging through the backlog from the October 1989 quake. With luck, they'll finish the paperwork on The Not So Big One before they have to deal with The Really Big One.

If your building is damaged, you'll probably need temporary space or a new location; you may need to move more than once. A company with several outlets can redirect business for the duration, but you might also approach another company about a mutual aid plan to share resources after a quake. If your business provides any earthquake-related service – a coach charter service or cellular phone retailer, for example – contact local emergency co-ordinators to let them know of your recovery plans.

You'll also need various repair services. So will everyone else in the business community, many of them with more clout and more cash. One answer is to write emergency response contracts with providers of essential post-earthquake services, for example security services, engineers, architects, various contractors and cleanup crews. Don't forget sources of funds. Dr. Charles Thiel says that all lines of credit could be cancelled after an earthquake until lenders know the status of affected businesses. Even as you recover, it may be difficult to borrow money for rebuilding. This is another good argument for careful hazard mitigation and a comprehensive insurance policy. Meanwhile, develop a financial contingency plan and discuss it with your banker.

It's an ill wind that blows no good, as the proverb says. Not only can planning enable you to resume business quickly, it can help you turn the situation to your advantage.

In a *Vancouver Province* story in February 1991, emergency planning experts said that, although many businesses failed after the Loma Prieta quake, some were notably successful. A clothing store filled a recreational vehicle with merchandise and sent it to customers unwilling to venture downtown. Home repair and remodelling contractors had more business than they could handle; governments were soon warning about fly-by-night operators. Trade was also brisk for office leasing firms, therapists and psychologists. Consider whether your company has anything to offer immediately after an earthquake or other disaster.

Profit needn't be the sole motive. In October 1989, Anheuser-Busch Inc. and several other California breweries immediately turned their production lines over to bottling sterile drinking water in cans. Cases of the cans were stacked on San Francisco area street corners within hours of the quake for people to take as they needed. They didn't charge a penny. Although they may ultimately have profited in positive public image, the breweries hastened to provide this public service at their own expense.

As a final note on business recovery, consider the matter of getting there and getting home. Unless your business is in the same building as your home, you probably trek to work by bus or car. If you ride a bike or walk, congratulate yourself on avoiding a nasty problem. If you live at any distance from your work, getting home from work after an earthquake could take you, quite literally and realistically, days of walking through disrupted and even dangerous areas. So could getting back to work to start recovery.

Now, not after the shaking stops, is the time to contemplate your transportation arrangements. Consider whether your work is separated from your living space by high tension wires, dams or reservoirs, rivers or other bodies of water, deep ravines, heritage neighbourhoods of unreinforced masonry or older wood-frame buildings, hazardous chemical manufacturing or distribution sites, or a significant distance.

Roads can fail in a major quake like the 1946 B.C. quake. A car eathquake kit should include the basic needs to get you to safety if you must leave your car and strike out on foot.

Buy the most detailed local map you can find, know the location of potential earthquake hazards, and consider altering your usual route to avoid danger. An earthquake could strike while you're in transit, and in any case will affect your speed and safety in getting home afterward. Earthquakes don't take time out for rush hour, any more than they do for the baseball World Series.

CHAPTER 5

SURVIVAL SKILLS

Curiosity and altruism may be humanity's two most endearing qualities. Disasters attract us irresistibly, but our primate curiosity is quickly overtaken by our compassion. A car crash is the classic example: people first rush to see the damage, then rush to aid the victims. Police officers and firefighters sometimes curse this interference, but the same two impulses also motivate heroes, saints and everyday volunteers.

Earthquakes are no exception to the disaster model. When the Interstate 880 in Oakland collapsed during the Loma Prieta earthquake, people who had been dealing drugs and stealing hubcaps minutes earlier became spontaneous heroes. Some used crowbars, carpenters' tools, anything they could find, to rescue trapped motorists – strangers all – from their smashed and burning cars. Others applied rudimentary first aid to keep survivors alive while ambulances threaded the wreckage-strewn streets. Fewer people would have survived without their willing hands and basic skills.

"Seventy-two hours" is the watchword for self-sufficiency after a major quake. You can expect to provide for all of your own fundamental needs including light rescue, fire control, first aid, warmth, shelter and food for at least three days. Emergency workers will probably be so overwhelmed by the numbers of people needing assistance, and by communications and transportation difficulties, that you'll effectively be on your own for the duration. Right at this moment you probably have most of the skills and capabilities you'll need to pull through the frightening, demoralizing and dangerous post-earthquake interlude. A few more can only enhance your overall competence at home and at work.

Any skills that you'll need after an earthquake are probably skills you can use in everyday situations and in any emergency. First aid, for example, is statistically more likely to be useful after household or traffic accidents than after earthquakes. You're also wise to know basic first aid if you have young children at home, or work with children or dependant adults. Many other earthquake-related skills could be useful in your work or recreation activities. If you're looking for a challenge and a change of pace, you can acquire or upgrade unusual skills. You'll meet new people, learn more about your community and provide a useful service.

Community organizations welcome volunteers, and will often provide suitable training. Emergency Social Services organizations, for example, depend heavily on volunteers. Salaried employees carry out only a few administrative functions; all other supervisors and workers are volunteers. Some municipalities are also encouraging creation of neighbourhood emergency response teams based on the police-sponsored Block Watch program. If you're not sure what's happening in your own municipality, ask the emergency planning co-ordinator.

These organizations emphasize training and carefully planned pre-assignment of volunteers. In any emergency, thousands of people turn out to help. They have a genuine concern for the good of others, they want to feel involved, it's exciting, they don't want to be alone . . . there are any number of selfless and selfish reasons for their participation. Emergency organizers regard these "convergent volunteers" as a mixed blessing. Most are untrained and, at that moment, all are unknowns.

Only so many well-meaning but untrained people are needed to carry plates in a soup kitchen or sort donated supplies. Too few volunteers offer their services in advance when their skills and interests can be put to the best use; too many unskilled and unknown volunteers flood in when there's no time to assess their capabilities and assign them properly. No wonder program co-ordinators tear their hair in frustration, and no wonder trained volunteers are worth their weight in gold.

Community organization volunteering may seem too structured or impossible to fit into your schedule. In that case, you can still work out informal arrangements with a few neighbours. If you have a registered nurse and a carpenter in your family, and your neighbour has outdoor survival training, you can all profit from pooling your skills in a disaster. Do avoid not knowing – or being unknown to – your neighbours at home or at work. Your survival and theirs may ultimately depend on co-operation. Midway through a major quake is no time to introduce yourself, organize and pool resources.

Every emergency program co-ordinator has a slightly different list of survival skills for earthquake response and recovery. City of Richmond co-ordinator Don MacIver's skills check-list for potential volunteers includes first aid and CPR, search and rescue, damage assessment, emergency shelter management, and operation of ham radio, citizens' band or walkie-talkie. These are the essentials, not only for earthquakes but for most foreseeable disasters.

A community response organization, however formal or informal, needs a thorough skills and resources inventory. Residents of Burkeville, a Richmond neighbourhood near Vancouver International Airport, recently formed the Burkeville Emergency Response Team (BERT) with the assistance of MacIver and graduate student Andrea Lacasse. Burkeville has a highly developed inventory and response plan because of its unusual setting and circumstances. The only residential community on Sea Island has only about a thousand residents, but as many as 25,000 people work and travel through the airport daily. BERT ambitiously thinks in terms of dealing with up to 30,000 people stranded by a disaster. As a result, its computerized skills and resources inventory covers more than 95 per cent of Burkeville households, and is extremely precise and detailed. Residents filled out a three-page questionnaire, not only of skills and resources, but also of family members' ages, daytime locations, medical conditions, interests, and work or volunteer experience. Because some information was sensitive, people were promised confidentiality.

The BERT inventory notes these skills: clerical, accounting, computer, training others, management, phones, radio operation, child care, food preparation, language, counselling, food serving, cleaning, carpentry, electrical, heavy equipment, plumbing, building repairs, personal assistant, first aid, CPR, medical professional, forklift operator, sorting materials, warehousing, directing traffic, truck driver, urban rescue, firefighting, and supervisory.

Only some of these call for extensive training. You may speak a second language as a matter of family habit, operate a computer or chainsaw by the seat of your pants, or care for children every day. Certain skills may be your daily bread if you're a crisis counsellor, health care professional, heavy equipment operator or carpenter. Others may be a natural byproduct of your present hobby, for example as an amateur radio operator. Even with everyday skills it's easier to establish who has them before an emergency than to ask around in the midst of a disaster.

A skills inventory is a natural first step toward a family or small business disaster plan. It's essential if you're thinking of taking things a step further to volunteer for a neighbourhood or community response organization. Start with your personal skills and training, then survey your family or co-workers' capabilities. You'll be surprised at the extent of your own skills once you put them on paper, and several people's usually make an impressive list.

Once you've done this, add three categories to each item on your list. First, are you already adequately trained in this area? Second, if you have a licence or permit, when will it expire? Third, do you need further training or upgrading? Now what you have is a chart that tells you at a glance where your skill strengths lie, and where you'd like to enhance them. The only thing remaining is to take courses or otherwise acquire the skills you want.

NO TRAIN, NO GAIN

Training for earthquake response or recovery skills is often available through night schools or extension courses. Community organizations may be able to help you with course fees if you're a volunteer. Here are some skills and the reasons for their usefulness after an earthquake.

First aid is your number one priority, whether you're responsible for your own family's wellbeing or an entire community's. After a moderate quake, you'll need only to stabilize injured people in the most basic ways until they can reach the hospital: make sure their surroundings are safe, get them comfortable and warm, check that their breathing isn't obstructed, stop any bleeding, and immobilize any broken bones. After a great quake causing widespread serious damage and injury, or with extra complications such as chemical spills, you may be unable to reach a hospital for several days. Ambulances won't be available either. You're on your own with your first aid handbook and your first aid kit. First aid training is not an option but a necessity if you're caring for children or dependant adults. Emergency specialists advise that at least one family member should take a first aid course. Courses can be as short as one weekend day, and are occasionally offered at no charge. St. John Ambulance offers a choice of excellent training courses, and needs volunteers for both routine and emergency duty.

Other medical skills may be important, depending on your circumstances. If a family member is a frail elderly or bedridden person, even one normally in care outside the home, home nursing skills are useful. Remember that after a quake you may have to practise them without electricity, water and sanitation. Cardio-

British Columbia's Provincial Emergency program helps catalogue the volunteer skills of thousand of coastal B.C. residents

pulmonary resuscitation (CPR), also available from St. John Ambulance, is a wise investment if a family member or co-worker has a known heart condition. Industrial first aid could be a good idea if you live in an unusually remote or hazardous location, perhaps accessible only by water, or work with heavy equipment or hazardous materials. St. John Ambulance offers this course, for which it charges several hundred dollars. Ask your employer to pay or share the cost, or consider this only for special needs or your own special interest.

Counselling is best handled by the professionals – psychologists, psychiatrists, social workers, clergymen or clergywomen – after a disaster. If you work in one of these fields now, consider further training in crisis counselling to deal with the common and often crippling post-disaster trauma.

Reception centres need volunteers trained in skills including food handling, shelter management, financial services and clothing distribution. Municipal Emergency Social Services gather and train volunteers in these and other skills, and drill regularly as part of their disaster planning program. Most are eagerly seeking volunteers.

Registration and inquiry, organized and provided by the Canadian Red Cross, is an important service during and after any catastrophe. The objective is to reunite families as quickly as possible afterward to reduce the trauma of separation, sweep away confusion and account for as many people as possible in the affected area. Working in a reception centre or other centre where emergency services are being provided, volunteers register all affected people and convey the information to a Red Cross head-quarters – in the Greater Vancouver area, to Red Cross House on Oak Street – and use it to answer all inquiries about the welfare of family members and friends. Call the Red Cross for more information about training and volunteering.

Light rescue after an earthquake has little in common with the mountain rope-rescues or helicopter airlifts of classic search and rescue operations. It might be more accurately termed "going out to locate and account for people." At its simplest, light rescue means combing a given area after a disaster to make contact with people, locate any injured or dead, and arrange to extricate any who are trapped. Municipalities occasionally offer training in light rescue; otherwise, the skills involved are mainly commonsense record-keeping and handyman skills. A neighbourhood inventory of who lives or works in each building greatly speeds the process.

Tunnelling and extrication takes place immediately after a quake. For the first day or two, the critical need is for people to carefully enter and partially dismantle damaged buildings to bring out survivors. This calls for people who can work with their hands, using tools available from any hardware store, in dangerous and cramped conditions. No claustrophobes need apply. Tunnelling and extrication is sometimes called heavy rescue, but this can give the impression that it requires heavy equipment. Cranes, bulldozers and other heavy machines can crush survivors trapped under building debris. Heavy equipment comes into play at the demolition stage long after all hope is lost of finding survivors alive in wrecked structures. Dogs are also useful at a later stage. "Dogs only find dead people, and I want living people," says Don MacIver. Tunnelling and extrication is best done by highly trained and organized volunteers, although training can be hard to find. Ask your municipal emergency co-ordinator whether it's available in your area.

Communications offer a lifeline after any disaster, especially one that interrupts telephone service. Amateur radio operators, citizen's band operators and walkie-talkie owners fill the gap. They may play one of several roles: passing on informal local-area messages, long-range radio communications, patching into emergency networks, or conveying packet radio (intense intermittent bursts of information to be downloaded and interpreted by computer). Amateur radio is licensed and governed by the federal communications ministry. Most municipal emergency programs have a "ham" network in place now, with regular drills and training, ready to serve its traditional public service function. British Columbia's Provincial Emergency Program (PEP) also has an amateur radio network which in a catastrophe would, among other things, link other existing radio services such as taxicabs, police cars and radio-equipped government vehicles. For information on training, membership and volunteer opportunities, contact PEP, your local emergency co-ordinator or your nearest amateur radio club.

Damage assessment is essential after a quake causes significant structural damage. Can people safely return to their homes or workplaces? Can they visit briefly to remove personal property before demolition or further assessment? Must the building be demolished immediately as a safety precaution? Architects, engineers and building contractors have the necessary skills to aid emergency teams in this capacity. Ask your municipal emergency co-ordinator for information on volunteering.

Repairs to damaged homes and buildings will be critically important almost as soon as the dust settles. These are temporary (plastic sheeting and plywood) repairs to create a liveable shelter, not complete and permanent repairs. The goal is to have people stay if possible in their own homes where they will be comfortable and secure, rather than crowding into reception centres or emergency quarters. Building contractors of any kind – plumbers, electricians, framers, rough or finishing carpenters, foundation or roofing specialists – are ideal repair-crew volunteers, since they already have the necessary skills. A community or neighbourhood emergency response organization can group them into teams and dispatch them where needed.

Security after a quake may offer mainly peace of mind, but that's not to be dismissed lightly. Although police forces and possibly even the armed forces (in the United States it would be the National Guard) will be responsible for personal and property security, a major disaster will tax their capacity to the full. During the summer of 1990, for example, the Oka crisis engaged most of the Canadian army's personnel and resources. Looting after an earthquake figures large in people's fears, but North American cities have actually shown a drastic drop in property crime for several weeks after a disaster. Community and neighbourhood groups can muster volunteer patrols, under careful supervision. Ask local police and your emergency co-ordinator about the suitability of volunteer security patrols, particularly in the crucial first 72 hours.

UPGRADE YOUR HOME

Make upgrading your home a family endeavour. Children can play a big part, and in the process learn the whys and hows of earthquake preparation. A child's-eye view of your home may give you some surprises.

- send children on a special low-elevation hazard hunt; give them stickers to mark locations of any unsecured furniture or smaller objects above the height of the smallest's head
- ask children to mark all cupboards and drawers in need of latches
- ask them to mark existing cracks or settling that need further investigation
- ask them to draw or list an earthquake-safe plan for their own rooms with attention to emergency exits, unsecured furniture or heavy objects, windows, mirrors.

Home earthquake safety measures for employees and their families will benefit everyone. You can:

- set up a communications network to create exchange post-quake information by a means other than telephone; designate communications points with radio or other communications where families can go for information
- consider providing CB radios or portable cellular phones to key employees
- hand out information on retrofitting, securing heavy furniture and objects, and other home safety measures
- hand out guidelines for developing a family emergency plan, with emphasis on an out-of-province contact person, permissions for children's release from school or day care, and family gathering places
- encourage employees to insure their homes and belongings
- provide guidelines or self-guiding booklets on preparing a home inventory
- develop and distribute an earthquake policy describing work expectations, emergency chain of command, and provisions for paying employees
- poll employee interest in buying home earthquake supplies at cost through the company
- consider providing home earthquake supplies to employees without charge
- stress earthquake survivability at home and at work

CHAPTER 6

YOUR EARTHQUAKE KIT

A year after the Loma Prieta earthquake, months after the dramatic television footage and newspaper features on earthquake preparedness, our survival supplies consisted of a can of sardines, an empty plastic bag and a case of canned fruit cocktail. It wasn't a brilliant beginning.

Food usually comes first to mind when people start collecting emergency supplies, as though we could starve within three hours of a disaster. Food is important, certainly, but it doesn't head the list. Our immediate survival needs are safety, warmth, shelter, water and then food, followed by intangibles such as companionship, information and reassurance.

If your home isn't substantially damaged by the quake or by fire afterward, you can stay there even without services until repairs are possible and things are more-or-less back to normal. You'll be more comfortable than in a motel room or a school gymnasium, you'll have privacy, you can start repairs and clean-up, and you won't be worrying about your pets or possessions in your absence. On the other hand, if your home is seriously damaged or a quake catches you some distance away, you may need safe shelter and warmth at least temporarily. Either way, you'll need personal items and survival supplies.

Commercially pre-packaged earthquake kits cost from about $100 to several hundred dollars each, depending on how many people they will supply and for how many days. They're ideal if you're short of time or uncertain of what you need in a kit. More suppliers are springing up all the time to meet growing public demand for earthquake and disaster kits. These kits may also include items that are easily overlooked or difficult to find, and aren't much more expensive than buying the same items separately. If you're in an isolated location, they may even be less expensive.

Commercial kits are not worthwhile if money is tight and you don't mind a few trips to the hardware and drugstore. Virtually every item in a commercial kit is available off the shelf, though perhaps in a less compact and appealing package. You can also substitute and make do if you're compiling your own kit, for example by providing your own bottled water and food instead of canned water and freeze-dried expedition rations. The bottom line is whether you care if your bag is eyecatching orange or pretty blue emblazoned with the legend "earthquake kit." A war surplus duffle bag works just as well.

HOW MANY KITS?

Some people have a "go bag" for quick evacuation, a fully supplied home kit, a mini-kit for each family member at work or at school, and a car kit. That can add up to at least four kits. Roy Sakata, the earthquake-conscious principal of John Diefenbaker Elementary School in Richmond, has a kit for each family member, his home and his car. Lynn Orstad of the Canadian Red Cross has three – home, office and car – because she's on the road so much and lives across a body of water from her office.

Orstad advises starting with the smallest and simplest: a go bag, also called a grab-and-go bag or an evacuation pack. This is emergency evacuation – as in fleeing imminent destruction – not a leisurely retreat. Remember, you could be injured or in shock. Firefighters estimate that occupants have two minutes to escape a burning house. Two minutes is long enough to grab the baby and (if you're lucky) your pocketbook, but you can forget about grandmother's sterling tea service. The same holds true after an earthquake if your home is seriously damaged, if you smell gas, if electrical current is arcing, or if the house is threatened by landslide or flooding. You might have 10 seconds to scrawl a note telling relatives or rescuers your whereabouts. At the door, you grab your go bag and you're gone.

If you don't keep an emergency kit in your car, take your go bag on day trips in case you're stranded away from home. In 1990 hundreds of skiers and travellers were stranded in Squamish by landslides on the highway; some went out for the day and got home two weeks later. A well-stocked go bag would have made life more pleasant for the duration.

Your likelihood of having to evacuate your home is low, especially if you make one purchase that can save you much grief and expense: smoke detectors and several good quality multi-purpose fire extinguishers.

Fire is the prime cause of damage after an earthquake, and probably the costliest and most traumatic. You should have at least one A-B-C rated (for all types of fires) dry chemical extinguisher on each floor of your living space, plus one in your car. Refillable extinguishers may be most cost-effective in the long term; ask your fire department for advice if you're not sure what to buy. Some fire departments also offer free courses and demonstrations on how to use extinguishers. Plan to attend.

If you can stay in your home, have avoided or extinguished any fires, and if necessary have shut off gas and power, you'll need somewhat different and more extensive survival supplies.

YOUR HOME EARTHQUAKE KIT

Earthquake survival style comes in a selection of green, orange or biodegradable, according to Lynn Orstad. The plastic garbage bag is beyond a doubt the mainstay of post-earthquake life. As rain gear, shelter, window covering, suitcase or privy, or in a score of other roles, you'll want plenty of them. You may even use some for garbage. The garbage bag also exemplifies the best news about your home survival kit: many of its contents are cheap or free, readily available, and highly adaptable.

Portability is not as critical for your home survival kit as for your go bag, since you probably won't be taking it far, but location is important. You'll want home survival supplies to be easily accessible and in a part of your house or apartment unlikely to suffer much damage. Some people suggest keeping them in a closet near an outside door; the closet will be sturdy because of its two-by-four framing next to a bearing wall, and relatively accessible from outside or inside the home. The real secret is keeping everything together so you don't have to hunt around a dark, possible damaged and dangerous, home. A front hall closet makes a good earthquake supply closet, and you'll still have room for coats.

A first aid kit is the heart of your home earthquake kit. You can compile your own or buy one pre-packed from the Canadian Red Cross, St. John Ambulance or a survival supply outlet. The cost will not be very great either way. Remember that you may not be able to get injured people to hospital for several days.

Warmth is your next need in any emergency situation, once you've established your safety. The greatest danger people face in an emergency is hypothermia, the dangerous lowering of body temperature. This is a hazard not only in the high arctic and on the high seas, but in the relatively mild climate of Vancouver Island and the Lower Mainland. Parks bulletins and public information campaigns continually stress the need for warm and waterproof outdoor clothing even on short hikes, yet every year a few people venture out lightly dressed, lose their way and perish from hypothermia. In British Columbia's coastal waters, anywhere beyond the warm shallows of swimming beaches, hypothermia will kill adults within about half an hour. Children, the elderly and the sick succumb even more quickly; infants and small children are terribly vulnerable because of their small mass.

Maybe The Big One will strike on a sunny weekend afternoon when you can stroll in from your back yard for a sweater. Or maybe it will strike in late December just as a vicious storm howls in past Cape Flattery, drives the winter neap tides over the sea dykes and upriver, and knocks out electricity and telephone, all at rush hour on a weekday. Flooding, gale force winds and bitter cold on top of a seismic disaster add up to a truly unpleasant few days, even death, for anyone who's not ready to fight hypothermia.

Hang a warm waterproof jacket, hat and gloves for each family member in your earthquake closet regardless of the season. Even clear summer nights get cool and damp after sunset in our climate. Don't forget comfortable shoes with thick socks. You never know how far you might have to walk. As you would for hiking, choose either waterproof or quick-drying shoes. Hats are especially important for children, whose heads are bigger than adults' in proportion to their bodies, and who lose body heat quickly through the face and scalp even in dry weather. Stuff a plastic supermarket bag – the kind with cutouts for handles – in each child's coat pocket. Vivian Johnson, a teacher at John Diefenbaker Elementary School in Richmond, developed the idea of using the bags to keep in body heat and keep out rain. This would be most useful after a summer earthquake, when children are unlikely to have warm coats and hats at school. She cut off one handle to improve vision. Do this only with constant supervision for young children, who can suffocate in plastic bags; normally you should keep them strictly away from lightweight plastic.

Damage could make your home unsafe, or fire could sweep the neighbourhood. In that case you might have to camp out, either in a park or in your own back yard, where you can keep an eye on your home and have access to its contents if damage is not too great. If you own camping gear, store the basics in your earthquake closet.

Blankets or, better still, sleeping bags for each family member can go on the shelf. They're lightweight and won't do any damage if a quake dislodges them. A tent, or plastic sheeting or tarp to improvise a shelter, will be useful. Store any other camping gear – air mattresses, lantern, cook stove – in the closet. People who are already familiar with backpacking, camping or outdoor survival, according to North and West Vancouver Emergency Program co-ordinator Ross Peterson, will stand the best chance of coming through earthquake aftermath in comfort and style.

Tools and materials to deal with the immediate effects of an earthquake, and for quick repairs afterward, belong on the closet floor. They tend to be heavy, and can cause damage or injury if a quake knocks them down. You'd never live down the embarrassment of being knocked cold by your own earthquake supplies! Start with a crowbar. You may need to pry open jammed doors to rescue trapped family members. Keep one of your fire extinguishers in your earthquake closet, too. It won't do you any good if you can't get to it because of fallen walls or furniture.

A whistle, the louder the better, can get the attention of searchers if you're trapped. Keep a sturdy pair of shoes under each family member's bed (since broken glass on the floor is almost inevitable and can cause serious lacerations) and a flashlight nearby. If your family includes physically challenged people keep a phone, whistle and flashlight in every room they use.

Some municipalities have been giving residents Help-OK sheets, letter-sized sheets of paper which are red (Help) on one side and green (OK) on the other. These are also easy to make by gluing together red and green sheets of construction paper, or by enlisting the help of an offspring with crayons. Placed in a front window or other prominent spot, they tell search parties at a glance whether or not you need immediate assistance. Some fire departments plan to give first attention to multi-family structures, where more people may be trapped or endangered, rather than to single-family dwellings. If you do urgently need help, you'll have to let searchers know.

Most other useful tools are household basics: hammer, screwdriver, pliers, shovel, axe, broom, goggles, work gloves, dust mask with filters. Several heavy-duty flashlights will be useful; at least one can be the power-failure type that recharges in a wall socket until the power dies, then automatically switches on. Others should be battery-operated, with plenty of extra batteries. The rechargeable kind run down after a few hours, and you'll have no way to recharge them since we probably face several days without electricity.

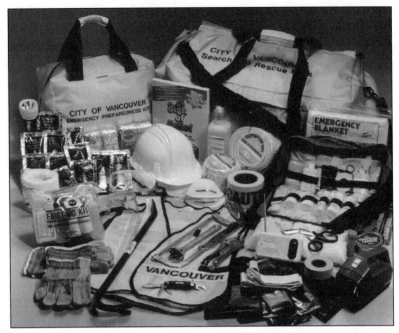

An earthquake kit can be as small as a bottle of water and a quarter for a pay phone, or as complex as the survival-rescue kits sold by several British Columbia suppliers. This one is from F.A.S.T. Ltd. Weigh the convenience of a pre-packaged kit against the flexibility of a do-it-yourself kit.

Useful materials include a good length of rope, a roll of duct tape, a roll of baling wire, and a roll of plastic sheeting. Nails or a staple gun with plenty of staples will also come in handy. Sheeting and duct tape can jury-rig a window repair or protect gaps in roof or walls from the elements. Naturally you'll want to make permanent repairs as soon as possible; so will several thousand other people. You may need to make do for a while.

Not everything you'll need after a quake will fit in a corner of your hall closet. You might want an annex in the garage, also near an outside door, or in a carport storage room. And some items belong instead where they'll be used. Your first concern – after the shaking has stopped and you've located family members – will be any indication of fire, gas leaks, electrical damage, and water leaks. Keep a wrench – either a standard crescent wrench or a specialized non-adjustable wrench – near your gas shut-off valve. Keep your wrench in a sealed plastic bag to prevent corrosion or freezing of the moving parts. Use it only if you smell gas; it may take many days for the utility company to turn gas back on.

After the Loma Prieta quake, 156,355 gas meters were turned off, 150,000 of them unnecessarily; although California's Pacific Gas and Electric Company borrowed service staff from four neighbouring states, it still took eight days to restore service. If your gas lines are intact, you might as well retain your gas service.

A fuse box or breaker panel controls your electrical power supply. It should be easy to turn off without tools if you smell burning insulation or see sparks. A rope ladder or, better still, a chain ladder with metal rungs, is a good investment in a multistorey home. Make sure it's long enough to reach the ground, and that you know where to attach it for a quick exit. If water is leaking in the house or a main seems to be broken outside, you'll need to shut off the water. Only if the valve is very stiff or corroded will this call for a crescent wrench or other tool.

A gas generator is essential if you need electricity for home medical support or other urgent reasons. These are not cheap; by shopping around you can find a portable generator for about $500, and a more powerful one for under $1,000. If you live on the Upper Island, in the Gulf Islands, or in any other area prone to power failures, you'll use a generator a few times every year anyway. Keep at hand at least one grounded multi-socketed power cord, preferably of 15 or 25 metres, and store fuel safely nearby.

SURVIVAL À LA CARTE

Power and other services are likely to be down for days after an earthquake, which will prevent you from preparing food using a range or microwave oven. Beware of turning to your fireplace or wood-burning stove. Chimney damage is extremely common in quakes; the 1946 Vancouver Island quake damaged about 50 per cent of the chimneys in several communities. If you light a fire when the chimney is breached, a house fire – without benefit of fire department – may add to your troubles. There's also the danger of asphyxiation. You'll need to have your chimney checked by a professional installer before you use it again. That leaves most of us using a barbecue, hibachi, camping stove or propane stove in a camper or van. Any of these is fine, used outdoors, as long as it doesn't depend on your domestic natural gas service like some gas barbecues. Don't forget to keep white gas, gas cylinders or other appropriate fuel on hand, preferably outdoors in a well-ventilated garden shed. If you're planning to use a propane-fuelled barbecue or camper stove, keep the propane tank filled through the winter instead of letting it run dry at the end of the summer. If you don't have a barbecue and don't want one, make a minimal investment in a foil roasting pan, a bag of self-starting charcoal briquettes and matches.

Water is your most critical survival item. It's probably the easiest and cheapest item to lay in before a quake and the most difficult to acquire afterward. Emergency experts say a healthy adult can usually get by for 24 hours without water, but all that time the body is using up its internal moisture and consequently dehydrating. The time will be shorter in hot or dry conditions, or for someone engaged in heavy work such as rescue or firefighting. Sick or elderly people, and especially infants and young children, dehydrate much more quickly and with more damaging effect. They need water regularly from the start. An adequate supply of clean drinking water, plus water for sanitation and other needs, is crucial to their survival.

You already have water in or near your go bag, but you'll need a more substantial supply if you're camping out in your home or back yard. The California rule of thumb is one litre of drinking water, plus another two litres of wash-up and cooking water, per person per day for at least three days and preferably for a week. For a family of four, that's 36 litres for three days. In British Columbia's moister climate, you may not need quite as much. A braced hot water tank can provide much of what you need. A few five-litre containers won't be especially portable but will be convenient, especially if you buy the kind with a spigot rather than a screw top.

You can easily and safely store ordinary tap water if you're prepared to recycle it about every four months. Buy milk or juice in plastic jugs for the next while to accumulate containers; you'll want to avoid breakable glass for this purpose. Clean them thoroughly with soap and water, then let them stand overnight filled with water containing a few drops of household bleach. Then rinse them thoroughly and refill with clean tap water. A freezer runs most efficiently when it's mostly full; if yours is usually half-empty, line the bottom with your earthquake water supply. Fill the jugs three-quarters full to allow room for expansion as the water freezes. A five-litre container will take about a day to thaw, and a one-litre container will thaw more quickly. Not only will you have pristine drinking water, but it will be served chilled.

Bottled mineral water will keep about a year in storage, and canned pure water will keep about four years. These are more convenient to stack than bottled tap water, and may also be sold in a more compact form. Canned pure water usually comes in flats of 24 cans, and the going rate is about $10 a flat. Mineral water prices vary. There are two other good arguments for buying canned water. It can be stored almost anywhere, since it can freeze and thaw without detriment to the contents or container. That means you can put it in a corner of the garden shed and forget it for four years. Also, after an earthquake, you can slide two or four cans into your pockets and walk away, instead of lugging a five-litre jug. Several bottlers of canned water are active in the Lower Mainland. You can also buy water in foil pouches which are equally convenient.

Food is not the great earth-quake-survival problem that people seem to think, unless you're in the unfortunate position of living day to day from a food bank. Most households contain enough food for days, if not weeks, in their cupboards, refrigerators and freezers. But in case your house is heavily damaged or your normal food storage areas are inaccessible – a kitchen after an earthquake is not a pretty sight – you'll need to keep some food in your earthquake closet.

Choose foods that store well without refrigeration, are easy to prepare and make up a reasonably balanced diet. Everyday canned or dried foods are fine. Buy food by the case when it's on sale, and cycle through it so that you never have out-dated foods in your closet. Don't forget baby food or supplies for family members on special diets. Stock your favourite foods (this is where we went wrong with our case of canned fruit cocktail; we've been hiding it in various concoctions for the last year, but it's amazing how long 12 unwanted cans can last). Since you probably won't have refrigeration, buy in small enough container sizes that you won't be throwing out leftovers or eating unsafe foods. When you contemplate quantity, remember that you may be feeding neighbours or relatives as well as your own family. The minimum amount in your closet should be the equivalent of three meals per person per day for at least three days. If you decide to add freeze-dried expedition rations, available from survival and outdoor stores, be especially sure to have enough water to prepare them. They're not cheap, but they keep well for an extended period and you won't have to recycle them as often as everyday foods.

Although you're not likely to undertake gourmet meals after an earthquake, you will need a few basic cooking utensils – perhaps spatulas and skewers for the barbecue, plus a few serving spoons – and plates and flatware for eating. Keeping your picnic set in the earthquake closet is one solution, but it might be easier to use plastic flatware and paper cups and plates. Paper towels and aluminum foil will be useful.

Your home earthquake kit is the place for medical or health supplies: vitamin tablets, dietary supplements, items for family members on restricted diets or with other special needs. These might include bladder pads, catheters, colostomy supplies, extra hearing aid batteries, hypodermics, white cane, or aids to comfort such as special pillows or backrests. Keep your doctor's name and phone number with these items, plus a note on prescribed dosages for all medications. Also, if you don't already have one, order a medical alert bracelet listing any medical conditions or allergies.

Pets are family members to many people. Free-ranging cats can usually take care of themselves after an earthquake and often vanish until things calm down anyway, but most pets need special care. It may be several days before you can get home. If you habitually leave an animal locked in a house or pen while you work, make provision for a neighbour to feed it in an emergency. Only guide dogs for the physically challenged are permitted in some emergency reception centres, and others may provide special areas for people with pets. Be prepared to make arrangements for your pet's care if you must evacuate your home. Letting dogs run free is out of the question. If they're running in packs, appear threatening, or are scavenging, they risk being shot by the authorities or by alarmed neighbours. Your earthquake supplies should include a week's food and water for your pet.

So far we've concentrated on physical survival needs for your home earthquake kit, but a few other items can make life more bearable in the short term and easier to resume later. Books, board games, cards, small hobbies and other entertainments will be invaluable if you're sitting out the aftermath in a back yard tent or reception centre. They're definitely worth the space, especially for children's games.

A small fireproof strongbox will set you back about $50. Here you can keep family identification, photocopies of all your credit cards, birth and marriage certificates, passports and deeds. Copies may not stand up in court, but if necessary they can help you to re-establish your identity. Have writing materials in your kit so you can write notes to searchers or family members if you evacuate. Computer backup disks or photocopies of essential paper files have a place here too, but be warned that strongboxes guaranteed to prevent paper from charring will not protect disks or other electronic media; these need a much higher fire rating. Photos of all family members belong here, not only for identification purposes but because they will ease your anxiety if an earth-

quake separates you temporarily. So also for important keepsakes, whether valuable or not, including baby mementoes, wedding pictures and heirloom jewellery. Since banks and automatic teller machines are expected to be out of commission for weeks after a major quake, keep some cash in small bills in your strongbox. You'll probably have to use it for most transactions until things get back to normal or until the government flies in new currency for the banks.

Weapons are not a wise addition to your earthquake supplies. There are always a few people who take advantage of others' misfortune, but you're probably safer in your house or a reception centre after a quake than you are crossing the street with a green light. Robbery generally falls off for a few weeks after a disaster. There's also the classic argument against weapons in the home: you or family members are statistically much more likely than an intruder to suffer injury from your weapons. If you feel you must have some means of self-defence such as a gun or a repellant spray like chemical Mace, don't even consider it unless you're thoroughly familiar with its operation and effects. Your best protection in any emergency lies in thorough security precautions and in keeping your wits about you.

Naturally your family won't need every item suggested here, but the list does add up to a bulky package. If your earthquake closet runneth over, or if you want to store things more transportably, consider packing some items in a duffle bag, large sports bag, retired toy chest, old steamer trunk, large backpack, or clean new garbage pail. If your neighbours see you pathetically foraging in a garbage pail for your meals, you may even get a dinner invitation.

OTHER KITS

You may want to cache a few useful supplies at your office, especially if you don't take your car to work. They should reflect two main concerns: getting safely out of the building whenever it comes time to leave, and getting safely home.

Flashlight with extra batteries, radio with extra batteries, and a few high energy snacks like granola bars or raisins are all easy to store in the back of a desk drawer. There should be a complete first aid kit in the workplace; if not, buy or put together a small personal one. A whistle could attract rescuers' attention if you're trapped in the building.

Comfortable old shoes, two pairs of thick socks and a map are your best aids to getting home. You may have to do it on foot, and that's a daunting prospect if you work in downtown Vancouver and live in Maple Ridge or White Rock. It will take several days because of damaged bridges and overpasses, and obstructions on the roads. Space permitting, you can add a change of underwear, a washcloth and small towel, toothbrush and travel-size deodorant. You could arrive home from a three-day urban hike looking no more frazzled than you do any Friday afternoon. Keep your supplies in a large plastic garbage bag, which will also give you emergency rain gear. Keep a few quarters in case you find a pay phone working.

Your car kit should fit in a small day pack. As with your office kit, its main functions are to keep you comfortable as long as you stay with the car, and to get you home safely once you leave it. Plan its complexity in proportion to the distance you normally travel to work, school or other regular destinations, and the potential hazards along your usual routes. A drive two miles to work along quiet Saanich roads won't call for the same emergency supplies as a drive across the Second Narrows Bridge and through industrial areas to Vancouver's office towers.

One important precaution is to always drive on the top half of your gas tank. When your fuel gauge hits the half-full line, refill immediately. It's better for the car, and the extra gas may be enough to tide you over. After an earthquake, service station fuel tanks may be ruptured, and gas may be unavailable or strictly rationed.

Keep a flashlight and a lightweight radio, both with spare batteries, for your trek. Add a detailed map showing the areas where you live, work and travel regularly. You may need to detour around disruptions and hazards if you leave the car to strike out homeward on foot, and you won't have time or energy for trial and error. Tissues and moist towelettes will be useful. Pack ready-to-eat food such as trail mix (raisins, nuts and chocolate) or granola bars, and bottled or canned water. Water is especially important if you have to walk home, since the exercise will dehydrate you more than sitting still. A space blanket and small first-aid kit are a good idea too. Have a pen and paper so you can leave a note in the car telling your name, destination and contact person. A red and green Help-OK sheet left in your car will tell searchers at a glance if you need immediate rescue or first aid.

Your all-purpose plastic fashion statement in green, orange or biodegradable will make an emergency raincoat or blanket. One hole in the bag's bottom for your head, two holes in the corners for your arms, and you have instant rain protection. Don't

Earthquake-generated soil subsidence and landslides can damage not only buildings but roads and railroads. After a 1959 quake, a 58 kilometre section of highway crumbled into a Montana lake, stranding more than 200 vacationers. Your car kit will help you if you're stranded by a quake.

forget a pair of comfortable old shoes. Now you know what to do with all your worn-out runners and casual shoes. If you have to walk any distance in high heels or stiff dress shoes, at every step you'll curse the day humans started to walk upright.

Consider also a mini-kit for school-age children (especially if they attend school far from where you work or live) containing at least some identification, a snack, the ubiquitous garbage bag, and the phone number of a contact person in case they can't reach you. Getting them to agree to carry this, let alone remember it, is another matter. If nothing else, have them write the contact person's phone number inside the cover of their notebooks. And make sure the school has an earthquake plan and well-stocked emergency kits.

One wonderful thing about earthquake kits and supplies, especially the ones you compile yourself, is that they're inevitably useful for minor household crises: tools, first aid supplies, temporary repair materials, flashlights, and so on. If you conscientiously recycle your food and water, keep batteries up to date, and generally keep tabs on your supplies, you'll easily weather emergencies that will beleaguer others.

Earthquake kits are the ultimate gift idea. Putting together a go bag or a home, car or office kit is a thoughtful and practical idea whether you're spending $10 or $1,000. Even for the person who has everything, an earthquake kit will come in handy for the executive jet.

CHAPTER 7

PLAN
TO SURVIVE

Earthquakes are survivable. Several times a year we learn that thousands of people have perished in earthquakes around the world. The headlines overlook that several billion people didn't perish. Luck saved a few; the rest survived through good planning.

"Seventy-two hours" is the password, an article of faith for emergency workers. If you can get through the first three days on your own, you're likely to make it through the whole experience. If you want to do this with minimum damage, injury and anxiety, start by drawing up a family earthquake plan (this could apply equally to roommates, co- workers or any other small group). The insights and procedures you work out will be useful day to day. On a mundane level, you may learn a more efficient way to drive to work; in a more abstract sense you may encourage your local government to operate more effectively. Your plan will also help you ride out any other kind of disaster from environmental catastrophe to civil disruption. Remember, you won't have time when the ground starts shaking to work out sensibly what to do next; you may be injured, in shock or trapped. And having an earthquake plan will give you peace of mind.

My favourite disaster planning story comes from Alberta, where a few years ago an emergency preparedness committee was just getting off the ground. All afternoon government and industry representatives proposed high-tech solutions to low-tech emergencies such as tornadoes and blizzards. No one paid much attention to the weatherbeaten older man who seemed a little out of place in the elegant boardroom; obviously the committee needed a farmer to represent rural interests, but he hadn't contributed much as the gathering prepared to break up for the day. At last the farmer got up and went to the wet-bar sink in one corner of the boardroom, reached underneath and turned a valve. Then he strolled over to the portable computer proudly displayed at the chairman's elbow, and pulled its power connection. Next he unjacked the telephone. Finally he went to the light switches. Suddenly the room plunged into blackness.

"Now," said the farmer's voice in the dark, "We've got an emergency here. No lights, no heat – it's forty below outside – no water, no phone, no food, and the elevators aren't working. Let's start planning for what we're going to do about it."

Once the lights came back on, the committee developed an emergency response plan that didn't depend on services that might not be available. Most important, it allowed for all the possible contingencies, and a few of the impossible.

FEET, DON'T FAIL ME NOW

A family council is an ideal time to draw up a plan, but if this never quite happens in your household, take a few minutes after a meal when you're all together. Plan on paper; in our information-oriented society, writing it makes it real. Make sure everyone in the family has a copy of the plan and keeps it where they can easily find it. Include children, even young children, in the planning process. Richmond school principal Roy Sakata, a groundbreaker in school earthquake preparedness, constantly reminds parents how much responsibility their children can handle. He tells of a four-year-old boy dialling 911 to bring medical aid for a stricken grandmother, and of children rescuing other people from fire and drowning. When it comes to assigning emergency tasks, children can also play a vital role. Above all, be sure your plan provides for the unplannable.

Sketch a floor plan for each floor of your home, showing all the rooms in detail. This may take thought and discussion, especially when you're identifying emergency exits and safe places in each room. Use the process to encourage everyone to size up every new room or area as they enter it, with special attention to places where they could safely ride out a quake.

Safe places are under a heavy table or desk, braced in a doorway with hands out of the way of a slamming door, braced in a hallway, against inside walls, or (if no other refuge is available) lying beside a higher piece of furniture such as a bed or table. Dangerous places are near tall heavy pieces of furniture, near heavy ornaments or other objects, near windows or mirrors, near refrigerators and other heavy appliances, or just outside a building where unsecured objects could fall on you.

"Most people are killed doing this 'feet don't fail me now' jazz," says Lynn Orstad of the Canadian Red Cross. "First they run out, then they run back, instead of just staying put."

BEFORE THE QUAKE

Divide your earthquake plan into three categories ₍ what to do before, during and after a quake ₍ to make the process easier and the results more clearly understood. What to do and when to do it are the essence of any emergency plan. Now is the time to decide what you'll need to do in preparation for an earthquake, break it down into tasks and assign the tasks to family members. Build in backups so that if one person isn't on hand to perform a task, at least one other person will know how. Allow for particular needs ₍ including a vital need for information, explanation and reassurance ₍ of the very young, the elderly, invalids, visitors or others who may have special difficulty dealing with a natural disaster. These people may respond much better in an earthquake if they know what to expect, what's expected of them, and that common reactions include lingering fear and anxiety.

Some municipalities reputedly give low priority to earthquake planning or other disaster planning. Don't, whatever you do, assume that in your area "it's all taken care of." Ask questions, and don't let anyone stall you off with inadequate answers; you pay these people to run your local government properly. The greatest responsibility for emergency planning falls to municipal, provincial and federal governments, but the greatest responsibility for ensuring that this happens falls to you as a citizen. Likewise, as a citizen you are responsible for getting yourself and your family through the first 72 hours until official emergency services take over.

You'll need to create four columns headed Task, Assigned to, Date completed and Date to repeat. Decide who will carry out each job, and when it should be completed and if necessary repeated. Get as many tasks as possible underway before your ink's dry, and be tough about the deadlines.

DURING AND AFTER THE QUAKE

Plan to find a safe place – ideally one of the safe places you've already identified in your home or office – and stay there until the shaking stops.

When it's all over but the cleanup, a written plan will again be helpful. Aftershocks can be stronger and more damaging than the original quake; be prepared to take cover again. You could be in shock or injured, and you will certainly be anxious to know the whereabouts and condition of family members.

You'll need to evacuate if your home is seriously damaged, threatened by unfightable fire or dangerous chemical releases, or otherwise unsafe. You may also be ordered to evacuate by police, fire or emergency crews.

Most important, run regular drills of the during and after phases of your plan. Canadians tend to dislike this kind of thing; we stand around shuffling our feet where our neighbours south of the border would be throwing themselves enthusiastically into the drama. One point draws agreement from all emergency response specialists: if you don't practise it beforehand, you won't be able to get through it when disaster strikes. Drills are also the best possible way to get any bugs out of the system so that it will run smoothly and effectively. Build the drills right into your plan, and make a family member responsible for rousting out the unwilling with bribes or threats, whatever it takes. Hesitation or fumbling in a real emergency could cost lives.

NEIGHBOURHOOD PLANS

The neighbourhood is the real extended family, some would argue, in our society of shrinking nuclear families, broken families, and non-family households. Yet in urban centres especially many people don't even know the names of their next-door neighbours. You could keep it that way and undertake your earthquake plans with a fortress mentality; you could prepare to be self-contained, neither seeking nor offering assistance in case of an emergency. But if you'd like to lower the drawbridge and drain the moat, earthquake planning offers a wonderful way to get to know and co-operate with your neighbours.

A neighbourhood earthquake plan is really just an extension of your family plan which lets you help yourself in greater depth and breadth, offer help to others, and expect help in return. It can be as casual as a chat over the fence or as formal as a government-sponsored emergency program like the City of Richmond's pilot project in the community of Burkeville. Informal plans take little work, but they also offer less assistance, and tend to drift apart easily. A formal sponsored structure can undoubtedly offer the greatest assistance in organizing, training, and assembling supplies and equipment. Contact your emergency co-ordinator for advice.

You may find, depending upon your municipality, that you won't need to reinvent the wheel to get a neighbourhood plan rolling. In North and West Vancouver, for example, the municipal emergency program is sponsoring individual neigh-

The 1964 Alaska earthquake devastated Government Hill School in Anchorage. The soil failure left a part of the school on unmoved ground and dropped the remainder into a wide trough. This quake could have been more tragic had it occurred during school hours.

bourhood emergency groups based on the existing structure of the RCMP's Block Watch program. Other areas have different structures. Each of these, at different levels, is an umbrella organization that embraces several smaller groups and functions. You can also take part indirectly by volunteering for different programs of the Canadian Red Cross, St. John Ambulance Emergency Social Services or other organizations active in your community.

A neighbourhood emergency group serves as, among other things, a central information bank of available skills, resources and equipment, plus the specific needs of residents. The Burkeville Emergency Response Team (BERT) compiled their information as a computer database after residents filled out a detailed questionnaire.

Before you head out the door with your clipboard and questionnaire, think about how you've defined your neighbourhood. North and West Vancouver's emergency co-ordinator Ross Peterson considers a residential block – usually housing fifty to a hundred people – about the right size for a community emergency group, and feels that a larger area could be unmanageable. Don MacIver, Richmond's emergency co-ordinator, thinks an area of several hundred people might be a little small. It's more than a philosophical question when you need to line up a good cross-section of skills and resources. If you can't reach a consensus about the appropriate size for a group, try starting with a small manageable unit such as a block. Leave well enough alone if your inventory turns up a good cross-section of skills, resources and equipment. If not, you can expand.

One further step remains. Although individuals and neighbourhoods are responsible for the first stage of earthquake response, there's only so much we can do effectively at this level. The government can't do everything, for logistical as well as philosophical reasons; full-time emergency response professionals such as police, fire and ambulance won't be able to reach everyone in need for the first three days after a disaster.

The larger neighbourhood is the city, then the province. Many people believe British Columbia's provincial government hasn't fulfilled its obligations. Federal matching grant money available to provincial emergency programs has gone almost unclaimed here because the province has allegedly been unwilling to contribute the necessary 50 per cent. In 1991 it received $1,500 in assistance of a total $4.7 handed out to all 10 provinces. The provincial government rationale is that any group in British Columbia – municipality, district, or interested agency – that truly wants to take advantage of the federal assistance can put up the matching funds. But local governments feel it's a provincial responsibility. Whose responsibility is emergency planning? Perhaps more voters should put that question to their MPs, MLAs and local councillors. It's time someone answered.

One critical need has been a set of comprehensive hazard assessment reports with plans for mitigation. Remember that a federal preliminary report predicted that a great quake would partly or completely destroy as many as 50 per cent of Greater Vancouver hospitals and schools. Essential services including hospitals, fire halls, police headquarters and Emergency Operations Centres (EOCs) above all must remain functional.

While planners and engineers have a reasonable idea of relatively sound and relatively unsound structures, we need more exact information on record in order to plan properly for emergency response. A City of Vancouver assessment of city-owned buildings was still under wraps at publication time; a similar study of other public buildings in Vancouver was near completion. But many thousands of people work and live in privately-owned buildings which have not been assessed.

School safety has drawn the most public concern. A Vancouver school board study found that nearly half of the city's 302 schools were at high or moderate risk – some of them century-old unreinforced masonry buildings – yet most are still awaiting provincial funds for desperately needed retrofits. Older or URM schools in other Lower Mainland communities and Greater Victoria also need upgrading for earthquake safety. Capital spending for schools is a provincial responsibility in British Columbia. As long ago as 1933, California recognized the importance of school earthquake safety by passing the Field Act to set safety standards for public schools. In a private letter, Vancouver lawyer Richard Watts wrote, "How tragic it would be for all of us if the loss of life and serious injury fell disproportionately on our children. No blow could be more devastating."

Even rapid policy changes bring slow results because of the high cost and labour-intensiveness of emergency planning. One thing is certain: if there isn't some rethinking, there won't be any results. As volunteer Dianne O'Brien said at one Burkeville meeting, "Shoot for the moon, settle for the stars, that's my motto."

DURING

Vancouver,
British Columbia

CHAPTER 8

QUAKE!

"Earthquake emergency plan is now in effect. This is not a drill. Follow your earthquake emergency plan. Repeat, this is not a drill."

These are not words you hope ever to hear – but there's a good chance that you will within your lifetime. You probably won't need a public address announcement to tell you that an earthquake is in progress. A great quake announces its onset with a rumbling that grows to a roar, like the sound of a heavy freight train approaching at high speed or like the thrum and shiver of Second Narrows Bridge at rush hour (as Red Cross worker Lynn Orstad points out). Then the earth will start to shake, perhaps violently, for anywhere from about 15 seconds to longer than five minutes. Length and strength of shaking are in proportion to the quake's magnitude, distance from the observer, and soil or rock conditions of affected areas. The 1989 Loma Prieta earthquake shook San Francisco for about 15 seconds, and areas closer to the epicentre for a little longer. The powerful Alaska earthquake of 1964 shook some areas of Anchorage for longer than seven minutes. The Big One, because of its expected strength, also could shake the ground for this long. The longer the ground shakes, the longer buildings and other structures sway, and the greater the damage.

The shock effect of the shaking alone, even without damage or injuries, is difficult to comprehend. You've probably waited for a jet to cross overhead so you can resume a conversation; it seems to take forever, but in fact takes about 20 seconds. By the end of several minutes of shaking you're either going to be thoroughly unnerved or, as one Alaska quake survivor claimed, thoroughly bored. A great quake may knock you off your feet with the first tremor, and you'll be lucky to crawl somewhere safe. One woman who experienced a mild quake near Prince George in 1986 had to stagger and lurch upstairs to her baby (it would have been better to wait until the shaking stopped). Even walking across a level room can be difficult during a quake.

You'll easily recognize a major earthquake; a moderate earthquake can be less identifiable. We felt a minor quake in

February 1991 in a shopping mall as a sharp shake and rumble, a pause of a couple of seconds, then a milder rolling rumble. Two employees' explanations seemed just as plausible as a quake: a heavy truck outside, or a repair crew working on the air conditioning. No one showed much concern. A great quake is unmistakable, and alarming.

What you do next depends on where you are when the quake strikes. A quake is most likely to find you at home, work or school, although you'll want to be ready for a spectrum of other possibilities. If you're in a familiar location for which you've developed a plan and drill, follow the steps of your drill as completely as circumstances permit, but be flexible; for example, you may need to choose an alternative exit.

In most locations, get under a sturdy piece of furniture. Hold on tightly, and move with it if it bounces around. That way it won't bounce on you, with luck, and objects on its surface won't bounce off your head. Then stay put.

After the shaking stops attract attention by shouting, banging the wall, flicking a flashlight on and off or any other means to get help. Expect more shaking from aftershocks, and interruption of all utility services including telephone. Now is the time to take advantage of your special precautions such as agreements with friends and neighbours to check on you in an emergency.

WHEN THE SHAKING STARTS
In some specific locations you can protect yourself further.

AT HOME
You're on familiar ground with relatively few hazards, especially if you've prepared carefully.

Your bed isn't a bad place to be during an earthquake. Pull up the covers and put the pillow over your head (probably what you'll wish you could do in any location during a quake.) Don't get under the bed; it could collapse. If there's no other safe spot in your bedroom, lie on the floor beside the bed and protect your head. Once the shaking stops, venture out for a safety check. Take your bedside flashlight and put on the shoes you've left under the bed to protect you from broken glass in bedroom and bathroom.

The kitchen, on the other hand, is no place to linger during a quake. It's full of heavy yet potentially mobile appliances, some of which could start fires, and it probably contains more breakables than the rest of your house together. If you're there when the shaking starts, turn off the stove and get out quickly before you're buried under a cupboard landslide. Usually there's considerable breakage in kitchens, even if you've secured your cupboards, and you don't need to add lacerations to your other woes.

Children at home create an added complication. Seek cover yourself while the ground is shaking and go to your children as soon as it stops. This probably flies in the face of all your feelings as a parent, but it's still the best plan. If you're injured trying to reach and comfort your children you'll frighten them instead, or fail them altogether. Protect yourself and go to them immediately after the tremor. You'll be doing the best thing for everyone.

AT WORK

Offices and other workplaces may contain heavy furniture or equipment that can be deadly if a quake sends it flying.

If you're working with machinery or potentially dangerous chemicals, try to shut down operations and quickly take cover under something sturdy like a table or workbench.

In a large boardroom, courtroom, lecture theatre or meeting room, either get under a table or desk, or kneel between the rows of seats. And stay there: that's the most important single recommendation for crowded areas. Do anything reasonable to discourage others from stampeding for the exits, but especially refrain from joining the stampede yourself. Many more people are injured by panicked flight than by remaining in a building.

Building type will have much to do with your overall safety. In most commercial buildings, the main seismic hazards come from furniture, lights, unattached objects and other non-structural elements. Modern office towers conform to seismic safety requirements in building codes, and are generally safe in earthquakes. Not everyone works in an office tower, of course. Mid-sized buildings of five to 12 storeys are usually relatively safe (especially recent buildings, since building codes improve markedly after each major Western Hemisphere quake), as are lower wood-frame or concrete buildings. Emergency planners worry most about older buildings with inadequate foundations, and especially about older unreinforced masonry buildings.

If an earthquake catches you in a high-risk building, particularly an URM, move immediately to an inside wall away from windows and get under a sturdy piece of furniture. Even if you know they're secured, get out of the possible path of flying or falling computers, file cabinets, light fixtures and other smaller objects. Even a flying stapler can injure you if it's moving at sufficient speed.

Don't use elevators during or after an earthquake, until they're checked by a qualified mechanic. Even after the shaking has stopped, elevators could be out of alignment or damaged in ways not immediately visible. Using them could be dangerous, and people trapped in elevators after an earthquake could be there for days while rescuers attend to more urgent cases. On the other hand, elevators are unlikely to snap their cables and plunge occupants to a terrible death. Multiple cables and counterbalances are designed to prevent exactly that kind of accident.

Eventually, after hours or even days depending on the extent of damage, you'll leave the building by a stairway or emergency exit. Don't rush to use these during or immediately after a quake. They may be obscured by smoke or dust, damaged, or jammed with panicky people. A stairwell stampede is extremely dangerous, and can cause deaths or serious injuries.

Under no circumstances should you leave a commercial building while the ground is shaking or soon after it stops. Bricks, stonework, awnings, window glass, roof parapets and an assortment of other architectural features become deadly projectiles during an earthquake, and most of them will fall near the entrances.

AT SCHOOL

Students should follow their earthquake plan exactly, even if the teacher's not there to lead it: duck under a desk or table, make sure their heads are covered and hold on until the shaking stops. If your child's school has no earthquake plan or regular drill, raise a commotion until the principal, teachers or school board develop one. Schools in British Columbia have copies of the publication School Earthquake Safety Guidebook, and should be formulating their own plans.

Encourage your children to be flexible if things don't go according to plan. If teachers are injured or missing, for example, they should still duck, cover and hold, exit calmly when the shaking stops, gather in the centre of a playing field, take a head count and administer basic first aid to the injured. Even young children can manage these steps if they're prepared and well drilled.

IN A HIGHRISE

Unsecured flying objects are usually the main hazard in a high-rise building during a quake. The building will sway, moreso in persistent shaking and on upperfloors. A California seismic design guideline suggests that a building's top floor will shake about twice as much as its base; in a 20-storey building the 15th floor will shake about one and three-quarter times as much as the base. Glass will break, tall furniture will topple and small objects will fly across rooms.

Expect a quake to interrupt electrical power and other services, and to trigger fire alarms and sprinkler systems even if there's no fire. On an upper floor especially, you may feel dizzy and be unable to walk across the swaying floor.

Move to an inside wall (preferably toward the centre of the building), get under a desk or table, and protect your head from falling objects and flying glass. Stay on your own floor. Don't use elevators until they're declared safe, and avoid stairs during or immediately after the quake.

IN AN ELEVATOR

Horror is bound to be your first reaction if a quake strikes while you're using an elevator. If you feel the building shaking, press all the floor buttons and get off at the first stop. If the elevator stops between floors, use the emergency phone or any other means to call for help. You may also be able to escape through the trapdoor in the elevator ceiling. If the shaking turns out to be a cement truck passing nearby and not a quake, remember you're better off wasting an embarrassed minute or two on the wrong floor than a miserable day or two in a dark elevator.

IN A MOBILE HOME

A mobile home can become too mobile for comfort in an earthquake. It's built to withstand more movement and shaking than any other kind of housing, but there's a limit to what it can take. Ground movement can knock a mobile home off its supports if it's not fully braced, causing serious structural damage to the entire home. When the ground starts to shake, follow the usual duck, cover and hold routine, and be prepared for a bumpy ride. Be prepared to check gas lines or other services as soon as the shaking stops, since they may be disrupted.

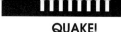

IN A STORE

Windows and entrances, usually with large expanses of glass and relatively little bracing, are the most potentially hazardous areas of stores. Tall display racks or islands are a close second, especially if they feature heavy, fragile items such as crockery or television sets. Avoid these when the ground starts shaking. Look for a table to get under, or crouch below counter level away from the cash register (which could topple) at a checkout stand. In large open-plan stores, especially in older masonry buildings, move to a pillar or an inside wall. Get down, hang on and protect your head. If you're a customer, follow staff directions to safe places and (eventually) safe exits. Many stores have signs or awnings over the doorways, so it's especially important to stay safely inside until the shaking stops.

IN A MALL

No one will soon forget the long, emotional and ultimately hopeless vigil for three workers in Santa Cruz's Pacific Garden Mall after the 1989 Loma Prieta quake. This and other collapses have left an impression of malls as disaster death traps. Pacific Garden Mall, however, was an area of heritage masonry buildings, which were beautifully restored but largely unreinforced.

Move into the nearest store if the ground starts to shake, get as far as you can from any windows, and take cover against a solid side or back wall. If possible get under a table or below the level of a sturdy display that won't rain objects on your head; then duck, cover and hold. If you have children with you, place them against the base of a wall and crouch over them as a shield. Protect your heads. Don't use stairs until the shaking stops and dust settles; don't use escalators, walkways or elevators until they're inspected and declared safe. Most of all, don't run for the exits. You don't want to get trampled in a panicky rush for the doors, and it's going to be much safer inside than outside for the next while anyway.

IN OTHER PUBLIC BUILDINGS

Overhead lighting and equipment may crash down around you. Stay where you are, get down between the seats or bleachers and stay there until the crowd can make an orderly exit. Getting crushed as others flee is your biggest single peril. Calmly follow any official directions about evacuation. You may have an overpowering urge to elbow others aside and surge for the exit. Stay put. Think of it as an exercise not only in restraint, but in survival.

OUTDOORS

Outside in an open area is usually a good place to weather an earthquake. Move away from power lines or anything else that could fall on you. If you're having trouble staying on your feet, sit or lie down.

A downtown street is another matter. Hurry into the nearest building or, if it's after business hours, get well inside an overhung entrance and protect your head from falling objects. Debris is a common hazard around large buildings. Flying fragments and sheets of glass, bricks, porticos, awnings, signs, stone facades or decoration can all kill or cause serious injury, especially if you venture out before the quake and immediate aftershocks have stopped.

IN YOUR CAR

In main thoroughfare or freeway traffic, pull to the side and stop well away from bridges, large buildings, overpasses and high-tension power lines. Cover your head with anything you can grab and get as low as you can inside the car. It will be your safest spot for the next few minutes.

Leave bridges, bridge approaches (often more unstable than bridges themselves), overpasses or tunnels without delay, but avoid high speeds that will endanger you or others.

Drivers caught on Oakland's collapsing Interstate 880 made desperate attempts to escape as the structure's sections pancaked one by one. Rescue crews later deduced that victims had swerved toward support columns, raced for the exits, or abandoned their cars to flee on foot. These panic measures failed to save their lives; most survivors escaped through sheer luck.

Traffic may soon resume in areas of little or no damage. Traffic signals will almost certainly be out of commission, and your greatest risk will come from other panicked and thoughtless drivers. After the shaking stops and you've surveyed your immediate area for hazards, proceed cautiously toward your home or another safe point.

Avoid any potential hazards you've identified on your route maps, including high tension wires, bridges, overpasses, dam floodpaths, hazardous chemical manufacturing or distribution areas, railway yards, heritage districts of close-built unreinforced masonry buildings, and large areas of landfill or bog. In some parts of Vancouver Island or the Lower Mainland, such detours could add hours or longer to your travel time. Eventually you may need to leave your car and continue on foot with your car emergency kit packsack. Leave a note in your

car giving your name, where you intend to go, a contact person, and any other pertinent information. Travel light in comfortable shoes with thick socks, and travel only by daylight so you won't stumble into danger.

IN A PARKADE

On foot, crouch down against a solid wall or pillar and protect your head with your briefcase, shopping bag, or anything else at hand. In your car, stop where you are – don't try to race for the exit – and get everyone in the car down as low as possible. If heavy debris falls, you will be safest in the part of your car below the level of your dashboard.

IN AN AIRPLANE

Thank your lucky stars, and hope that your luck stretches to provide an airport to land at. Several coastal British Columbia airports could sustain damage ranging from fissures or sandboils in runways to submersion caused by sudden sea level changes. Expect an emergency landing.

ON THE BEACH

Folklore claims that a few years ago when a northern Vancouver Island town received a tsunami warning, many residents went straight down to the beach to wait for the tidal wave. Someone brought a radio, someone else lit a beach fire, and soon a party was in full swing. It promised to be the biggest excitement since the school burned down. The RCMP did not appreciate this festive spirit.

If you're on or near the beach when an earthquake strikes, ride out the quake where you are, getting under cover and protecting yourself from flying objects. When the shaking stops, don't linger to admire the scenery. Warning systems will probably give time for orderly evacuation, but be prepared to scramble.

My parents' house upcoast, once a bunkhouse floated from logging camp to logging camp, still has functional wooden skids hidden behind its foundation skirting. Most waterfront houses lack this amenity. Your best response to a tsunami threat or the first suggestion of changing surface levels is to grab the go bag and bolt for higher ground. If you've never seen film footage of a tidal wave, borrow a videotape from your local library showing a tsunami in Japan, Chile or Hawaii. The force and speed of the water's onslaught are terrifying, irresistible and vastly destructive.

Column supports failed on Interstate 880, allowing the two road decks to "pancake." Rescuers worked for days to pull out injured and terrified survivors, never knowing if the structure would collapse further. Several major overpasses and bridges have recently been upgraded to meet higher seismic safety standards.

ON A BOAT

Afloat is one of the best places you can be during an earthquake. Far offshore, you won't even know about the quake until you turn on the news.

Closer inshore, you may need to ride out any waves generated by the earthquake or by underwater landslides. Places to avoid in a boat (if you've picked up an earthquake report or tsunami warning) are close to unprotected shores, in shallow bays, at moorings or tied up at dock. If you're close to shore, beach or moor in a hurry and run for high ground. Otherwise, try to get into the lee of an offshore island or inside a sheltering bay or inlet. If you can't do any of these things, head straight offshore as far as you can safely venture, steer into the waves and ride out the swells. Prince Rupert fishermen did this during the tsunami warning a few years ago – a false alarm – fearing their craft would be dashed ashore as fishboats were in the 1964 Alaska quake.

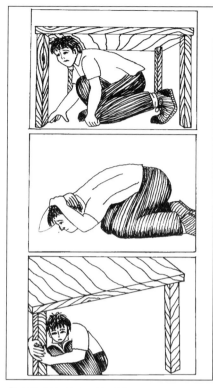

Duck, cover and hold.

Find cover.

OTHER PLACES

Quickly leave hazardous locations where staying put won't guarantee your continued wellbeing or, for that matter, your continued existence: heavy industrial areas, chemical plants, refineries, railway yards, high tension wires, neighbourhoods of unreinforced masonry buildings, dams, sea causeways, bridges and bridge abutments, overpasses and tunnels. Can you safely duck, cover and hold? Or would you be safer to run? You'll have to make a split-second decision.

DUCK, COVER AND HOLD

Remember these three words above all. Relatively speaking, everything else is an embellishment.

Psychologists say that you may feel better about the whole experience – one small human can reasonably feel puny pitted against global tectonic forces – if you count slowly, snap your fingers or tell the earthquake to stop. Eventually it will obey.

Cart horses were among the first to perish in San Fransisco's devastating September 1906 earthquake. Thousands of people died or were injured in the quake and the great fire that followed.

AFTER

CHAPTER 9
SEVENTY-TWO HOURS

Silence, darkness, stillness: the first moments after the shaking stops are the eye of the storm. All hell will break loose almost immediately, and it will last for days. Your first reaction may be to exit your home or workplace at a run, but stay put. You could run straight into a hail of falling debris.

Stay in the eye of the storm, stay calm, while you gather your thoughts. An extra minute won't make a difference in most situations but will help you to recollect your personal earthquake response plan so you can proceed step by step without hesitation. At night you'll need the shoes you left under your bed to safely cross areas of broken glass, and your bedside flashlight. Don't turn on electric lights yet; if you have a ruptured gas line, the spark as the circuit closes could ignite gas fumes. For the same reason, don't under any circumstances use a match, candle, kerosene lamp or any other open flame.

Take a head count of everyone in your home or work area. Account for everyone, note whether people are injured, and evaluate their psychological state. You'll need to know whether people are in shock or otherwise incapable of coherent thought and action before you do anything further. If possible, gather them into one safe area.

Now quickly assess the overall condition of your home or surroundings. Is there serious damage? Is there any immediate danger, especially from structural collapse, gas leaks, potentially toxic chemical spills, other explosion risks, or fire?

If there's any hazard, evacuate people immediately to a safe location such as a reception centre, taking go bags and other emergency supplies with special emphasis on first aid needs. If there's no discernable hazard, make people comfortable indoors. They may be there for a while, since it's probably the safest place available.

Next do what you can to halt or prevent the building's destruction. Operate as though no one will be along to help. This is a safe assumption: no fire department, no utility repair crews, no police, no ambulance. Fight fires with your fire extinguishers.

If you don't smell gas and have no other reason to believe there's a gas leak, leave the gas valve alone. If you smell gas, primarily near the water heater, furnace, other gas appliances or gas lines, use your wrench to shut off gas service. Then open the windows and doors, and carefully leave the house. It may be days or weeks before you can get a repair crew to reconnect it (when it is reconnected, remember to relight all pilot lights). Quickly check your electrical power; if there's any suggestion of damage – sparks, a hot insulation smell, damaged fuse boxes or breaker panels – shut down your power and don't use it again until it's professionally repaired. If you encounter downed power lines near your home or workplace, stay at least 10 metres from them to avoid electrocution.

Injured people need immediate attention once you've established that the building isn't going to burn or explode. Apply only basic first aid at this point. Make people comfortable by ensuring they're warm – especially if they're in shock – under a blanket or coat. Keep them quiet. Don't try to move them if they appear to have serious injuries, particularly neck or back injuries, unless they're at risk from fire, falling debris or some other hazard. Stop any bleeding with sterile bandages or other clean cloths. Immobilize broken limbs. Ensure that breathing passages are clear. These are elementary steps in stabilizing patients until help can arrive – but after a major earthquake help may not arrive for days.

What you do next will depend on the severity of the quake, the seriousness of injuries, and your proximity to medical treatment. After a devastating quake, if you're suddenly cut off from the nearest hospital by distance or physical barriers and your patient clearly needs more than basic comforts, you may have to apply more intensive first aid. Now your first aid training and first aid handbook come into use. Start by checking carefully for concussion, breathing obstructions, foreign objects in eyes or wounds, depressed skull fractures and other grave injuries. Administer pain killers if necessary. Proceed with caution, and do only what you must to maintain life and keep the injured person comfortable.

Psychological treatment may also be needed. Some people can't handle even routine functions after a disaster, and may need special care and counselling. This is especially true of young children, the ill, the mentally or physically challenged, the frail elderly, and the newly bereaved. People separated from their families may also be anxious to the point of helplessness. But don't assume all children or all elderly people or anyone else will automatically be incapable. Not only may they be fully capable, they will almost certainly benefit from keeping busy and taking positive steps to get conditions back to normal as quickly as possible. You won't be in a position to offer truly dysfunctional people a great deal: companionship, relative safety, reassurance, perhaps minor tasks.

Children in school will quickly need your attention. You'll want to pick them up immediately, but that may not be possible. After a serious quake police may ban all but emergency driving until roads and utilities are repaired. You may be separated from the school by a downed bridge or overpass, fires or other hazards, or simply by distance. If one child attends a school several kilometres away and you have a pre-schooler at home, it could be a major undertaking to set out on foot through unknown conditions. It may be less frightening and less dangerous for all concerned if you leave your child in the care of the school for as long as a few days. This underlines the absolute necessity for schools as well as families to have workable, well understood, regularly drilled earthquake plans.

One Saanich elementary school, for example, lays out exactly what the school and parents will do after an earthquake. The school will keep children under supervision for up to 72 hours, until a parent or other authorized adult claims them. An authorized adult who is not a parent must be identified on a pre-signed release form on file at the school.

Parents are asked neither to phone the school, as all lines will be needed for emergency communications, nor to drive to the school, because roads must be kept clear for emergency vehicles such as ambulances and fire trucks. If they must drive, they should park at least four blocks away and walk in to claim their children and any others they're authorized to collect. They're asked to check in at an information post in the middle of the playing field, and not to remove any child without notifying people at the information post. They should bring jackets in case children have been evacuated straight from the classroom.

The emergency plan at Cumberland Junior High School, attended by rural as well as town students, also takes into account possible traffic jams. Many parents will have to drive in to collect their children because they live at some distance, yet routes must be kept clear for emergency vehicles. The school's answer is simple: no car will be allowed into the school parking lot.

Driving, if not banned outright, is not a good idea after a major quake. Sightseeing is especially inappropriate; this is one time to suppress our natural curiosity. Roads and nearby structures may be dangerously damaged, high voltage power lines may be down, tidal waves may be about to strike (you should especially avoid any waterfront areas either on foot or in a car), or toxic chemicals may be leaking. At best you risk unnecessary injury. At worst you can cause traffic congestion and block the passage of emergency vehicles. San Francisco's devastated Marina District in October 1989 drew such a plague of sightseers that some enraged homeless residents assaulted the gawkers. Only emergency workers belong in stricken neighbourhoods. Bereaved and dispossessed people deserve their privacy – and remember that you could be one of those bereaved and dispossessed.

Take care of family health from the start. Make sure everyone takes prescribed medication, especially those with diabetes, heart disease or other potentially fatal conditions. Get plenty of clean water to drink. Eat regularly, starting a few hours after the quake with a ready-to-eat snack such as a granola bar and fruit juice. Don't try to live on coffee and jam sandwiches for days; you'll pay for it by being jazzed up, stressed out and undernourished. After enough of this mistreatment, your body will start drawing on its stored protein and other nutrients, weakening your resistance to fatigue and illness at the time when you can least afford it.

After you've dealt with injuries and stress as well as you can, clean up any spilled liquids or other substances. Some could be flammable; others (such as ammonia and bleach) can react together to release toxic fumes or explode. A few could simply be a nuisance, like sticky maple syrup that tracks across your floors.

Your pets will need attention, too. Administer first aid if they're injured. This is not as easy as asking a human to sit still while you dab disinfectant or remove glass splinters. The human may yelp, but probably won't bite. Your unfortunate dog, cat or parakeet can't understand this sudden torture by a beloved owner. You'll need to muzzle a dog or hold a cat's mouth closed, and wrap the unaffected parts in a towel or blanket to protect yourself from a mauling. Don't give aspirin to dogs, cats or other pets; it can cause serious reactions. Even unharmed pets will probably need comforting and reassur-ance. Animals have a longstanding reputation for unpredic-table behaviour associated with quakes. For their safety and the safety of others, confine pets until life is back to normal.

Having done all you can for your family or companions, next venture out to see if anyone living or working nearby needs similar help. Elderly or disabled people, or families with young children, may appreciate your assistance or even the simple knowledge that someone's aware of their presence and concerned for their wellbeing. You may also be able to pool resources, skills and equipment. Communal cooking for three or four families can save fuel, offer welcome company to people with the jitters, occupy time, and give children a sense of normal activity.

Aftershocks often strike again soon after a major earthquake, and can occur for several days before they dwindle to nothing. Sometimes aftershocks are more powerful than the initial quake, and cause more serious damage. In the three weeks after the Loma Prieta quake there were 4,760 aftershocks, but only two were strong enough to cause damage. Most were weak enough to be imperceptible to humans. An aftershock can endanger lives if it topples an already unsound structure while rescuers are trying to free trapped victims. Rescuers and volunteers crawling between the collapsed levels of the Interstate 880 in Oakland never knew when another tremor could crush them along with the earlier victims they were trying to extricate. Always assume that there will be aftershocks, and be ready to take the same precautions as for any quake. It would be irksome to survive The Big One with flying colours and succumb to The Hiccup.

ON SECOND THOUGHT

Your first thought, and everyone else's, will be to phone your family or friends. First make sure all your phones are on the hook. You may be unable to get a dial tone or place a local call. The telephone system can handle only so many phones being engaged at one time, either because many calls are being placed or because a quake has knocked many receivers off the hook. In emergencies, a system of ranking calls comes into play. Emergency response professionals' and some volunteers' telephones have this "priority listing," as do pay telephones.

If you have an emergency, try your phone. You'll probably get a dead line with no dial tone when you pick up the receiver, but don't hang up. There is an outside chance that you'll get a dial tone after a few minutes as other calls cycle through. If so, keep your emergency call brief. But your chances of making a local call are slight. Cellular phone networks may function, but they remain a relatively unpredictable resource.

Since your odds are better of getting a long distance line than a local line, you could well reach your designated out-of-province contact person long before you reach family members across The Gorge or Burrard Inlet. Your out-of-province contact should be unaffected by a west coast earthquake. You can also help clear the phone bottleneck by making one brief long distance call instead of several local calls. Phone your contact person as soon as you can get through, pass on full information about your own circumstances – injuries, deaths, damage, evacuation – with a request to relay this to other family members or friends. Eventually everyone should know each others' whereabout and circumstances, though it may seem strange to find out from New Brunswick or Saskatchewan. This may take several anxious days.

Next you'll need information in a general sense. Emergency measures may be in effect. Health officials may be advising that you boil your drinking water, or evacuate certain areas because of toxic chemical leaks. Police may have banned driving of motor vehicles. There may be announcements about restoration of electricity, natural gas and water service. A tsunami warning may be in effect. Radio always comes into its own during fast-breaking news situations and emergencies. Radio reporters can cover and broadcast the news within minutes; after a disaster, other media may have to wait days before they can broadcast or print. Also, while a few people have battery-powered television sets, a majority have battery-powered radios.

You'll also need to provide information by placing your red and green Help-OK sign in your front window or another prominent spot visible from the street. The red Help side will tell emergency crews at a glance if you desperately need first aid, rescue or other immediate assistance. The green OK side will announce that you need no immediate help. This simple act will save much time, and that time may save the lives of trapped or injured people. If you must evacuate or leave your home, you'll also want to leave a note for family members giving your whereabouts and other pertinent information.

Water for various uses will be your number-one survival need. Check your plumbing to see whether water pipes and drains are functioning, and whether you have water pressure. Pour cold water into your bathtub if there's water in the pipes; this can be your wash-water. Also investigate your hot water tank. Unless it has fallen or ruptured, it should contain all the wash-water a family of four would need for several days. Either source, preferably with boiling or other purification, could also supply drinking water. Other sources of water are any canned or bottled water you've stored for this kind of disaster, the plastic bottles of frozen water in the bottom of your freezer, the water in your toilet tank (unless you've added a disinfectant this is clean water, unlike water in your toilet bowl) and the contents of your refrigerator ice cube trays. Go easy on the water, using no more than a litre per person per day for drinking and two litres per person per day for cooking and sanitary needs; you don't know how long it will take to restore water service or to truck in emergency water.

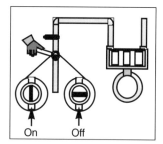

Know how to control your gas valve.

If drains aren't working, don't allow any use of toilets. Otherwise you may discover dangerous, bacteria-laden human waste accumulating in your basement or back yard or, worse still, under your floorboards. An outdoor latrine may be your safest short-term solution if you have a place to dig one. Dig a trench or hole a metre deep, and use a tarp or plastic garbage bags attached to poles to create privacy. In an apartment, turn your toilet into an arctic style honeybucket, with a kitchen-sized plastic garbage bag draped inside the bowl. You can apply lime, as in provincial campgrounds, to fight bacteria and reduce odour. Tie bags tightly and double-bag when you're discarding them, and label them as human waste. Personal cleanliness is essential, including careful handwashing in hot soapy water after using the toilet. Children may regard a disaster as a great adventure, but don't relax standards of cleanliness now. A bad case of dysentery is miserable under normal conditions; without hospitals or antibiotics, it could be fatal.

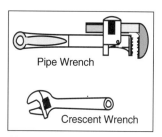

Know your wrenches – pipe wrenches are best for big jobs while crescent wrenches are easier for small jobs. Keep one of each handy.

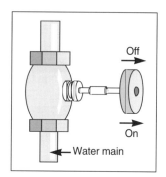

Make sure you know where your water shut-off valve is and how to operate it in an emergency.

Secure your home against intruders as soon as possible if you suddenly have gaping windows or unlockable doors. Looting and burglary aren't usually a problem after a quake, but why make a it too easy? Nail plywood or boards across doorways or windows with easy access, especially if you must evacuate. At the very least, nail up plastic sheeting to keep out weather and marauding animals.

Eventually you'll want to prepare meals. If the only damage to your home is temporary loss of services, start by eating the food in the refrigerator before it spoils, then work through the food in the freezer as it thaws, and next eat the food in your cupboards. You'll need some means of cooking. If you have a full propane tank or good supply of charcoal for a barbecue, you'll be fine for days. Remember to use it outdoors only, since the barbecue represents a fire hazard and the fumes can be toxic. Your natural inclination may be to try your alternative heat source, probably a wood-burning stove or fireplace, but these rely on chimneys to carry off fumes and heat, and chimneys are frequent victims of earthquake damage. Using a fireplace with a cracked masonry chimney or a misaligned metal pipe chimney can lead to fire or asphyxiation. Wait instead until a qualified installer can check your chimney and if necessary repair it. Meanwhile, cook outdoors even if it means vaporizing the Queen Anne chairs to grill your ground round. Better them than you.

Lanterns take cautious handling, too. A white gas lamp can be used indoors only with a window open, for example, and even so you're better to use it strictly outdoors. Flashlights are a better bet in every way, since they'll operate as long as you have batteries. Rechargeable flashlights that you leave plugged into your wall sockets are fine for the first hour of an emergency, but they soon fade away. I discovered this when I spent most of a recent power outage both cursing the darkness and lighting candles.

Once you pass through the emergency stage to some semblance of calm, check your home for non-critical damage that you overlooked in your first rapid assessment. List your damage and expected repairs. Distinguish between repairs you can easily carry out with tools and materials on hand, emergency repairs you can make until professional repairs are possible, and difficult or major repairs beyond your skill. Note doors that won't open or close, shattered windows, cracked plaster, separated walls or porches, broken utility lines, fallen masonry or trim and – perhaps most important – damaged foundations. Otherwise some earthquake havoc may come to light only much later (as my cousin Marquita discovered to her dismay a full year after the Loma Prieta quake), robbing you of the opportunity to make an insurance claim, or to repair it and prevent further deterioration.

A ROOM SOMEWHERE

Far away from the cold night air is the place to be when the sun sets and the insects rise. Even summer nights are cool in this climate. Protection from the elements is important for adults, and essential for frail elderly people and children. While there's still daylight, to save yourself discomfort at best and dangerous hypothermia at worst, take shelter.

Ideally, you'll be able to stay in your house even if you've had to make emergency repairs to doors, windows, walls or roof. You'll probably be more comfortable there in familiar surroundings than in a temporary shelter outdoors. Life without the utilities we take for granted – power, water, gas, telephone, garbage pick-up – may not be a lark, but is certainly liveable.

Life without a habitable house is less appealing. Outdoor living takes on a whole new meaning when there's no indoors to return to. Some resources may be usable, though, even if your home is heavily damaged. You may be able to lock some possessions in your garage, make full use of all your camping gear, drive your car eventually, get regular changes of clothing, have bathroom privacy, use the foods and utensils from your kitchen, make repairs and start cleaning up.

"Muddling through" best describes this back yard camping. My grandfather excelled at it, having lived off an inhospitable land twice, as a scout in the South African War and in the trenches of the First World War. A camping trip to the Oyster River with the Padre, I'm told, was a revelation in bivouac tactics. After pitching camp, he would comb empty campsites for discarded tin cans, planks, twine, any small treasure to improve the quality of life. By the next morning his tent would have a wooden floor, extra guy ropes and maybe a rain fly. A day later he would have a mirror fragment to shave in, a dented but serviceable feed tub to take hip baths, a cook stove fashioned from a discarded oil drum to heat the water, and all shipshape and tidy. After a week, he would start making his famous hashes of bully beef, crackers, potatoes, eggs, and anything he could barter from a nearby farm. After two weeks he would tie on a clean dishcloth apron, sterilize a dozen homeless bottles, and make pickles. After a month, his fishing camp looked like a squatter's homestead. He always left with a touch of regret, but started anew the next summer.

If you have a tent or you can jury-rig a lean-to, you can probably muddle through for quite a while in your back yard. But you may not have the choice.

Fire, heavy damage, chemical spills or other hazards could force you away from your home entirely. Radio bulletins will notify you of your nearest reception centre, and advise what to take with you. Many emergency reception centres are secondary schools or recreation centres, since these have the space, kitchens, toilet facilities and other resources necessary to handle a large number of people. Pets cannot always be accommodated, except guide dogs for the visually impaired, but will not be left hungry or homeless. After the 1989 Loma Prieta quake, the American SPCA operated an "adopt a pet" program, billeting homeless pets with volunteer families until their owners arranged accommodation. Informal arrangements took care of many other pets.

Typically, in a limited emergency affecting a few hundred people, reception centres will offer mainly registration and inquiry, personal and financial services: Red Cross volunteers will solicit personal information to pass on to inquiring family and friends; medical professionals and trauma counsellors will treat those in need; government representatives will provide financial assistance if necessary. Homeless people will be housed elsewhere, probably in nearby motels and hotels, eat at local restaurants with meal vouchers, and receive a change of simple clothing such as a track suit from a local store.

A major disaster affecting many thousands of people remains a relatively unknown quantity. One Lower Mainland emergency program, for example, provides for the creation of more than two dozen reception centres to deal with victims of a major catastrophe – in theory. In practice, the program has only enough volunteers and resources to operate one or two centres (if you're waiting for a reason to volunteer for emergency programs, look no further; you're almost certainly needed).

If you must go to a reception centre after a quake, take your go bag, important personal effects, and a change of clothing. Just don't expect all solutions to your problems to arrive on a silver platter; the centre may be understaffed and sketchily organized. Remember that these dedicated volunteers have left their own families to come to your aid. They deserve your respect and patience as much as you deserve theirs. It shouldn't be necessary to remind anyone of the golden rule, but volunteers sometimes experience hostility and even violence from distraught victims.

Intangible aid may be the best thing a centre offers in a crisis. There's plenty of care and compassion even if physical comforts are lacking. People respond to disasters in different ways, ranging from deep depression and listlessness to near-hysterical giddiness and gallows humour (within hours of the Loma Prieta quake, San Franciscans were dancing in the streets by candlelight and joking that the collapsed two-level Interstate 880 was now the Interstate 440). Human company, assistance with material concerns including insurance claims and banking, counselling for grief or trauma, children's activities, impromptu recreation and shared activities can help victims through their immediate post-quake anxiety. That's only the beginning, of course, for people who are seriously traumatized. They will need professional help.

A visit to the reception centre, whether for coffee and a doughnut or for a week in residence, can let you catch your breath before you get on with recovery. Sometimes encountering others with more grievous losses helps us to bring our own problems into sharper focus.

TRUTH AND OTHER RUMOURS

We live in an information society, but our information flow is largely electronic and instantly vanishes when the plug is pulled. From being information-rich, we're suddenly information-starved. Since nature abhors a vacuum, the breach is quickly filled by quasi-information such as rumour. Rumour soon gives rise to confusion and fear.

Information and misinformation are among the post-earthquake realities. We might as well be prepared to deal sensibly with rumour and its ugly consequences. Consider a frightening story from Edmonton's 1987 tornado, which killed residents and destroyed homes in the Evergreen Trailer Park, among other areas. One trailer park resident who suffered relatively little loss owned a bookstore specializing in occult and metaphysical works. She was accused of calling down the tornado by malicious rumour-mongers – someone repeatedly vandalized and defaced her home with spray-bombed religious threats, and destroyed her bookstore in several arson fires. She had been accused of calling down the whirlwind by malicious rumour.

Less exotic but unnerving rumours can describe post-disaster epidemics of cholera or typhoid, many deaths kept secret by authorities, people left buried alive in building rubble, widespread looting and assaults, summary shooting of looters (guilty or otherwise), and other assorted horrors. After the 1906 San Francisco quake, a few of these actually did occur. Most were only rumours, yet some are amazingly long-lived.

Fact is the only real remedy. The Red Cross's registration and inquiry program puts survivors in touch with each other and

informs inquiring outsiders of their status. Amateur radio operators and volunteer couriers provide the first emergency information, mainly to disaster workers and Emergency Operations
Centres. Radio, and eventually television, newspapers and maga-
zines, traditionally provide essential coverage and bulletins within hours or days. The Loma Prieta quake also generated
commercial videotapes and books which, months afterward, told
survivors what they had in part experienced and told outsiders
what they had escaped. This provided an important aid for victims trying to get back on an even keel. All these information services can be invasive, sensational and exploitative; but they can
also provide a vital community service. Perhaps the wisest
approach to information from any source is to take all with a grain
of salt until you can verify it. A disaster is no time for blind faith.

Waiting is the hardest part of the post-quake period,
whether you're at home or in emergency shelter, especially if
your family is scattered and out of communication. This is the
time when you'll want your family photos as a reassurance that
eventually all will be well.

WE MADE IT

The worst is over, broadly speaking, 72 hours after an earthquake.
The aftershocks and fear of aftershocks have dwindled to a tolera-
ble level. The dust has settled, the smoke has cleared, the injured
are in hospital, the hungry are fed, the homeless are sheltered. You
know what you've lost and you know what you've saved.

Reunions with family members, friends, neighbours, even
pets are likely at this stage. At the bare minimum you should
know their status; with luck you'll be back in your home and getting on with life. American Red Cross registration and inquiry
workers, 72 hours after the Loma Prieta quake, had successfully
processed so many calls that they reportedly had only 12 further
investigations to carry out for people inquiring about the safety of
family and friends. Considering the extent of disruption – 63 people died, 3,757 people were injured, more than 12,000 people were
left homeless, nearly 4,000 businesses were destroyed or damaged – having only 12 people unaccounted for after three days
indicates the phenomenal success not only of the program but of
our ability to bounce back from the most terrifying experiences.

CHAPTER 10

MOVING ON

Getting your life back to normal, at least back to pre-quake conditions, will be uppermost in your thoughts. Experienced recovery workers warn that you won't fully achieve this goal.

"Life will never be quite the same for all those people; even their language has changed to mark the big event – now they talk of life 'before the quake' and 'since the quake,'" writes Rev. John Hill of the Uniting Church of Australia, who aided 1989 earthquake recovery efforts in California. A major disaster changes lives and alters communities, and its shocks will be deeply felt for years.

Recovery is the least understood, least documented and least prepared-for aspect of disaster planning, yet most emergency coordinators consider it the most important. Hill stresses that recovery is not a phase but a set of activities concurrent with other post-quake activities. "Recovery begins at the moment of impact."

Material loss and physical damage are the most visible effects of a quake, and generally speaking the easiest to remedy. Moving home, cleaning up, arranging repairs, going back to work or school are all fairly manageable. Damaged buildings including apartments and single-family dwellings (as well as business and government buildings) will need inspection and approval before they can be reoccupied or rebuilt. Knowing the economic and psychological cost of homelessness, California municipal officials made heroic efforts to do this quickly after the 1989 quake. Nevertheless, a months-long backlog delayed homeowners and tenants from putting their lives back on the rails. Some people endured far worse predicaments, of course. Many were now homeless; others lost not only homes but all possessions, important documents, even personal identification.

Emotional and psychological reactions demand more time, effort and sensitivity. Residents of San Francisco's heavily damaged Marina District had this nightmare experience: when they returned to their buildings after the quake, which struck at 5:04 p.m., most were denied entry by police, firefighters or other officials. The area was cordoned off until the next morning, when hastily assembled building inspectors and engineers began examining buildings with an eye to their safety and reparability. Green, yellow and red tags – and similarly colour-coded identification cards – denoted buildings that were safe for reoccupation, in need of further assessment or repair, or unsafe and marked for immediate demolition. After sleeping at an emergency shelter or in a nearby park, residents queued to re-enter their homes. All of this took place under the hungry gaze of curiosity seekers.

Those with green tags could reoccupy their homes and begin clean-up and repairs. Those with yellow cards could enter accompanied by an engineer or inspector, usually for 15 minutes, to remove their most precious possessions; reoccupation might be possible later. Some of these people were so badly shocked when they re-entered and saw their personal wreckage that they emerged after 15 minutes empty-handed.

Those with red cards were refused entry. Their homes and all their contents would be torn down, bulldozed and reduced to landfill. For people already frightened or injured by the earthquake, this was a last devastating blow. Some were so distraught that police had to restrain them physically.

Possessions are not only material objects, they're the reflecting surfaces of your life and experience. Those you lose will be hard to forget, forgive or replace. But – once you have lost them – list them carefully, make an insurance claim, focus on what you have left, and get on with your life.

MOP AND PAIL

Cleaning up after a disaster is an essential step, perhaps even a rite of passage, as anthropologists describe a ceremony to mark transition from one stage of life to the next. It will make your home liveable again by removing hazards and obstacles, putting things back where they belong, removing the hopelessly damaged, setting aside the salvageable, and making an inventory of the replaceable and claimable. More important, cleaning up is your first major act since the ground started shaking that reasserts your control over your life. Even if money is no object, carrying out your own clean-up will give you a sense of accomplishment. Work as a family team, giving each person a task. Children, who are especially vulnerable to disaster trauma, gain confidence and security from contributing visibly toward recovery. As long as you're looking at toppled furniture or shattered crockery, in a sense you're still in the grip of the quake. Once

you've cleaned up, you've truly survived the earthquake's shock, loss and fear.

Start your clean-up with bathroom, kitchen and bedrooms, the most frequently used areas in most homes. Broken glass and spilled liquids may be the worst damage your bathroom sustains, and most bedroom furniture and fittings aren't especially destruction-prone. But at some point you'll have to steel your nerves and venture into the kitchen, typically a scene of whole-sale earthquake destruction. If your cupboards have latches, open them carefully; crockery, glassware and canned foods may be leaning against the inside of the door ready to fall. If there are no latches, the cupboard contents will already be decorating the kitchen floor and walls. Clean up spilled foods first to reduce odour and spoilage. Throw out any contaminated or doubtful foods; most perishables will spoil after a few hours at room tem-perature. Don't risk food poisoning. Many garbage bags later, you should see daylight in this task. Then go on to other rooms.

Start putting together an insurance claim now, guided by your household inventory list and any photographic or video-tape record of your possessions. Take your time over the list, since it will be difficult to make a second claim for the same dam-age. Your insurance agent will be swamped in similar claims; expect delays in processing and payment. If you don't have insurance, make a claim to PEP or any other government agency which is co-ordinating compensation for earthquake damage. After a major quake, public restitution may be small and will almost certainly be long delayed, as it has been after floods and other British Columbia disasters.

Repairs may take a long time to secure. Any great quake will damage thousands of homes and other buildings. Contrac-tors are likely to respond first to businesses and individuals with clout, prior contracts or fistfuls of cash. Kindness does occur, though. When the 1946 quake damaged many chimneys in the mining town of Cumberland, near Courtenay, the coal company sent crews to repair the company houses. The mineworkers, always a close-knit community, agreed among themselves that families with small children or invalids would get their chimney repairs first.

Such generosity may spring up again, especially in areas where people know each other, since disasters seem to bring out people's best behaviour. Nevertheless, you'll be wise to repair anything possible yourself, even if you do a jury-rigged job with plastic sheeting, duct tape and wire. With luck it will hold until you can hire a qualified contractor.

Quickly assess the damage, even if you can't arrange immediate repairs. If you're unaware of the full extent of your damage,
you don't need any surprises after you've filed your insurance
claim. Also, some problems such as foundation damage may be
invisible at first to the casual observer. A simple, inexpensive
repair a few weeks after a quake can become a complicated, costly repair a year later.

Avoid quick fixes. The Fly By Night Fix-It Company may
well hit your doorstep in person or with a flyer, offering cut rates
on quick repairs. Last week your instant building contractor or
plumber could have been selling shoes, and may know less about
repairs than you do. Botched work and repair scams have
plagued Californians after several recent quakes. Flim-flam
artists prefer easy prey, especially the elderly, lonely and
bereaved. Deal with businesses you know, if possible, or businesses accredited under the Better Business Bureau or a professional association. Check credentials, sign nothing on the spot,
pay nothing until the work starts, and if necessary take advantage of the British Columbia law that gives you seven calendar
days to change your mind and withdraw from any contract
signed in your home, away from the contractor's place of business. Don't forget to apply for all necessary building permits and
inspection when you make a permanent repair; without these
you could be ordered to remove the reconstruction.

LIFE GOES ON

Returning to normal after a disaster can be a long slow process
for anyone, but some people traditionally fare better than others. Among those who recover most easily are the well
informed and the well heeled; they know what to expect before
and after an emergency, and they're not forced to scramble for
their daily necessities.

Emergency planners have observed for years that disaster
does not change people's circumstances, but accentuates them.
People with good resources, support systems, health and energy
will struggle with adversity and survive, although they will be
more aware of their vulnerability, writes Rev. John Hill. "On the
other hand, those who were disadvantaged before the disaster –
because of age or illness, shortage of money, lack of a job or a home,
personal circumstances, or frayed social support systems – will
have found that what was once bearable has become intolerable."

Our present system favours the strong and punishes the
weak, Hill adds. While individual people show compassion,

there's little sign of it in the policies and plans of government. Governments tend to perceive recovery as a phase – a delayable phase – and to heavy-handedly dispense aid such as shelter, food, clothing, financial assistance, and some mental health counselling. Then they withdraw, leaving behind chaos and dissatisfaction. Hill stresses the need instead to plan well in advance for a flexible, timely and fair network of recovery programs directed not by a government representative but by the victims.

"The ultimate goal of disaster recovery is to enable creative renewal in the life of the community and its members," he writes, "but all the good will in the world cannot make that happen if there are no plans for it."

Disadvantaged people suffer the greatest loss of life, damage and anxiety in disasters like earthquakes. They are the main occupants of substandard housing, especially older unimproved wood-frame buildings and unreinforced masonry buildings. Coastal British Columbia, like California, has plenty of these structures. More than 50 per cent of the living space destroyed or seriously damaged by the Loma Prieta quake constituted low cost housing or hostels. The disadvantaged may also lack the material and personal resources to recover easily. In British Columbia this group could include the physically or mentally challenged, ill, unemployed, illiterate, frail elderly people, new Canadians, illegal immigrants, substance abusers, people on social assistance, and the economically threatened working poor. They are unlikely to have earthquake insurance or any other insurance. Their lives are difficult before an earthquake, and disastrous in the aftermath.

Helping disadvantaged people to recover from a disaster is expensive because of their greater material and psychological needs. Do yourself a favour as a taxpayer, if not for philosophical reasons. Lobby today – not when it's too late – for more and better housing for the disadvantaged, and tougher legislation to encourage identification and retrofit of unreinforced buildings, both public and private. Demand non-punitive, non-stigmatizing support for those in need. Call for education and self-development assistance to enable disadvantaged people to improve their lives.

LOSS AND GRIEF

Fear and uncertainty, grief and anger, follow any major earthquake. No one is immune. Those who have lost family members, homes or jobs have a tangible reason to be upset; others have good reason to fear they will suffer similar losses in the inevitable next quake.

AFTER

As many as 25 per cent of people may be incapable of coping with the effects of a major earthquake, one emergency planner estimated. California Red Cross workers after a 1987 quake said that up to 40 per cent of their contacts needed referrals for crisis counselling, and that typically these people were not seeing counsellors for other personal problems; they were part of the "normal" general population.

Since no great quake has struck coastal British Columbia in living memory, we must look elsewhere to predict the psychological effect. After several recent California earthquakes, some adults felt depressed, unable to concentrate, jumpy, numb or immobilized by hopelessness. Some were unable to sleep, lost their appetites, or suffered from headaches or fatigue. Others were angry or anxious about the earthquake's disruption of their activities and relationships. Some grieved for lost friends, family members or possessions. Older people seemed reluctant to discuss their losses or anxieties, perhaps fearing loss of their independence. New arrivals from Latin America who were survivors of other quakes were particularly fearful; many slept in parks although Red Cross shelters were available, and didn't want to return home. Police, firefighters and other disaster workers also showed the strain and needed debriefing.

Linda F. Fain and Diane Myers of the California Department of Mental Health stress a need for people to inform themselves about likely reactions to earthquakes. "Knowing what to do before, during and after an earthquake helps minimize the trauma that can result. Reducing the potential destruction to one's property and possessions can correspondingly decrease the misery one must bear. People who know what kinds of emotional problems can be caused by earthquakes will be both less likely to be confused and disturbed when they themselves start having them, and more apt to seek intervention when a problem is serious."

Two particularly high-risk groups emerged after the 1989 Loma Prieta quake.

Recent immigrants shared the fears and grief of other Californians, but also distrusted government agencies and feared that they would be deported if they accepted disaster relief. The earthquake also reawakened their memories of earlier traumas including natural disasters and wars. Any difficulties these people experienced were aggravated by language barriers and, in many cases, by poverty. Emergency workers had already identified immigrants as groups that would need special services, and quickly co-operated with ethnic outreach services to provide

126

assistance and offer public education information in Chinese, Spanish, Vietnamese, Thai, Cambodian, and other languages.

Women in California experienced the same earthquake-related anxieties and trauma as other people, but no one anticipated another disturbing phenomenon. Santa Cruz reported incidents of rape, sexual assault and domestic violence – including the area's first gang rape case and three murders – rose sharply about 10 days after the 1989 quake and remained high for several weeks. Sexual assaults rose 300 per cent, according to a report to Santa Cruz's mayor by its Commission for the Prevention of Violence Against Women. When one crisis line resumed operation, calls were up by 25 per cent. Not all callers described recent violence; many were re-traumatized rape and incest survivors for whom "the earthquake brought on the same sense of powerlessness that assault causes."

Some men used the earthquake as an excuse to resume old relationships; some women remained in dangerous relationships because of housing or emotional problems caused by the quake. A director of Men's Alternatives to Violence reported that "men seemed angry at women for their feelings of fear." He also cautioned against a tendency for emergency workers to see family violence as "a trivial priority, condoned under the circumstances," compared to conventional survival needs such as food, water, first aid and shelter.

Child abuse also increased, especially by parents who already had difficulty coping; traumatized children now demanded extra attention which parents were incapable of giving.

Responses were swift. Child protection agencies offered child care and counselling to parents and other caregivers in an attempt to limit abuse. An information campaign soon warned Santa Cruz residents of the connection between stress and violence, and how "the fear of being out of control can lead to the desire to exercise control over another person."

Children can be incapacitated by fear and grief after earthquakes, and need special help to get through a frightening experience. After recent California quakes, some children showed regressive behaviour such as crying, clinging, screaming in the night, bedwetting and thumb sucking. Some had nightmares and difficulty sleeping. Others were easily frightened by loud noises, quick movements, even by curtains blowing in a breeze. Some became more aggressive or withdrawn. Many were afraid of going back into their homes, even if they were only slightly damaged. School work suffered as older children had trouble concentrating, take tests or listen to teachers. They were too immersed in their unhappy feelings.

Young children usually don't understand natural disasters or the resulting human problems; all they know is that their parents are injured or missing, their homes are damaged, their play groups or school routines are disrupted, and the people they love and trust are themselves sad, afraid or irritable. All this causes emotional upset, and can lead to permanent emotional damage.

Fear underlies all these reactions: fear of separation from the family, fear of death or injury, fear of another earthquake, fear of being left alone. These are all reasonable fears under the circumstances; after all, if parents and other adults are visibly frightened, why not children? Children need reassurance and explanations.

Mother Nature has a big yawn and stretch sometimes, and that's what makes the earth shake, Lynn Orstad of the Canadian Red Cross tells young children's groups. This usually explains earthquakes to their satisfaction. A lecture on seismology is usually the last thing they need. What they do need after a quake is plenty of understanding, attention and love.

You should know soon if you're unable to help your children get over their fears on your own. Don't take this as a sign of failure; you're not alone. Seek professional help through your family doctor or health clinic.

Children or adults who suffer bereavement need to acknowledge their feelings and go through the natural grieving process. Some people manage this with the support of family and friends; some need professional counselling. As with children's trauma, the longer you suppress grief in all its complexity, the longer it will take to heal.

Healing will take place eventually. Survivors of many disasters have said in various ways: Until this happened, I never realized how wonderful it is simply to be alive.

THE BIG ONE: AN EARTHQUAKE SURVIVAL GUIDE

All the good intentions, all the promises, will be the first casualties of the major earthquake that certainly faces us in coastal British Columbia within the near future. Basic planning and preparation can save your home, your livelihood and your life.

Dire predictions are wasted breath. Thousands of people who didn't prepare at all survived the Loma Prieta and Mexico City earthquakes without a scratch; the odds are still better if you do prepare physically and psychologically.

Since you've taken the important step of informing yourself by reading *The Big One: An Earthquake Survival Guide,* you already know you're a survivor!

(The following pamphlet has been reprinted here in its entirety, with the kind permission of the San Fernando Valley Child Guidance Clinic).

COPING WITH CHILDREN'S REACTIONS TO EARTHQUAKES & OTHER DISASTERS

This pamphlet has been prepared to help parents deal with children's fears and anxieties following a disaster. When we use the word "parents" here and throughout the pamphlet, we are also including teachers and other adults having responsibility for the child.

THE EARTHQUAKE

The February 1971 earthquake was one of the most dramatic and unpredictable events that had ever occurred to many children in

the Los Angeles area. They were awakened at 5:59 a.m. by a frightening shaking of the earth, their beds rocking – sometimes moving across the room, furniture tumbling over, walls rattling, toys falling off the shelves. In many instances they saw their parents upset and frightened and perhaps clutching them.

An earthquake is a "natural disaster." Other such events are fire, flood, or tornadoes. These are traumatic or frightening events that may occur is some children's lives. These events result in families having to leave their homes and familiar surroundings. A child does not usually understand such events and feels confused, anxious and frightened.

In the concern for the physical safety of the child and family, attention to and awareness of the emotional consequences to the child are frequently neglected. We cannot control these events. However, they need not result in permanent emotional damage to the child.

UNDERSTANDING THE CHILD

The course of growing up for the average child consists of certain regularities. For most school age children regularity involves the presence of parents, awakening in the morning, preparing for school, meeting with the same teacher, the same children, playing with friends, sleeping in his own bed, essentially being able to depend on a series of predictable events. The child expects a dependability from adults and certainly from the forces of nature. For the pre-schooler life is much the same. He spends his day within the familiarity of his world, be it at home, with babysitters, or a nursery school, etc. His family remains more or less constant. When there is an interruption in this natural flow of life, the child experiences anxiety and fear. How the adults help the child to resolve these "problem times" may have a lasting effect on the child.

FEAR AND ANXIETY

Fear is a normal reaction to any danger which threatens life or well-being.

What is a child afraid of after a disaster?

He is afraid of recurrence, or injury, or death.

He is afraid of being separated from his family.

He is afraid of being left alone.

Parents should recognize, however, that these are fears that stem from within the child, his imagination or his fantasies, as well as those fears that are stimulated by a real event. Even after the event has passed, his anxiety will sometimes remain. The child may not be able to describe his anxious feelings. Even though he is intensely afraid, he may be genuinely unable to give an explanation that makes rational sense.

The child, who is dependent on adults for love, care, security – even food, fears most the loss of his parents and being left alone. In a disaster, even the child who is usually competent and unafraid may react with fear and considerable anxiety to an event which threatens the family. Since adults also react emotionally with normal and natural fear to disaster, the child becomes terrified, taking parental fears as a proof that the danger is real. A child having less experience in distinguishing a real threat is likely to be plagued by fears with no basis in reality. It is important to note that fantasied danger can be as real and threatening as "real danger."

A child experiences similar fear in other situations; for example, when parents separated, or divorce, when a child goes to the hospital or when there is a death in the family. Parents all recognize these more familiar fears and attempt to deal with them.

In natural disasters like fires, floods, tornadoes, or earthquakes, our first concern is with and our first attention goes to physical safety. This is as it should be.

However, parents tend to ignore the emotional needs of the child once they are relieved that nothing "serious" has happened to members of the family.

When there has been no physical injury, they may be surprised about the persistence of the child's fears. They may even feel resentment, particularly if the child's behavior disrupts or interferes with the daily routine of the family.

One must recognize that a child who is afraid is afraid!

He is not trying to make life more difficult for himself or his parents. His fear is uncomfortable to him. He would like nothing better than to be rid off his fears. If the child feels that parents are not understanding of his fear, he feels ashamed, rejected, unloved and consequently, even more afraid.

A first step for parents is to understand the kinds of fear and anxiety a child experiences.

Parental understanding and helpful intervention can reduce the severity of fears and can prevent more serious problems from developing. This is not a new role; parents routinely and effectively help children cope with fears encountered in day-to-day situations. However, when an unusual situation occurs, the ability of some parents to reassure their child, particularly when they themselves have been frightened, may be impaired. The child feels even more fearful or anxious when suddenly he is unable to turn to the adults for reassurance.

ADVICE TO PARENTS

What can parents do to help their child? It is of great importance for the family to remain together.

Being together with the family provides immediate reassurance to a child. Fears of being abandoned and unprotected are immediately alleviated. For example, immediately after a disaster parents should not leave the child in a "safe" place while they themselves go elsewhere to inspect possible damage. They should not leave the child alone in the evacuation center while they go back to the damaged area; they should not leave the child to go shopping, but should take him along. With no opportunity to experience the fear of being left alone, the child is less likely to develop clinging behavior.

The child needs reassurance by the parents' words as well as their actions!

"We are all together and nothing has happened to us."

"You don't have to worry, we will look after you."

Realistically, parents are also experiencing fear. However, they have the maturity to cope with the stresses upon them. A demonstration of strength should be apparent to the child who will feels more secure and reassured; however, it will not harm the child to let him know that you are also afraid. As a matter of fact, it is good to put these feelings into words. This sharing will encourage him to talk about his own feelings or fears. Communication is most helpful in reducing the child's anxiety and, for that matter, the adult's anxiety. The child may then express some fears which are not real and the parents will have an opportunity to explore these fears and reassure the child.

Listen to what the child tells you about his fears.

Listen when he tells about how he feels, what he thinks of what has happened.

Explain to the child, as well as you can, about the disaster (the fear inducing event), about the known facts and, again, listen to him.

A child may express his fears in play or in actions. If these are unrealistic, explain and reassure him. You may have to repeat yourself many times. Don't stop explaining just because you have told him this once before.

Encourage him to talk.

The silent child needs to be encouraged to talk. His difficulty in expressing himself may be very frustrating to the parents. It can be helpful to include other members of the family, neighbors, and their children in a talk about reactions to the disaster. Through the sharing of common experiences, fears are further reduced. It is essential that an attempt should be made to provide an atmosphere of acceptance where a child will feel free to talk about his fears (be it at home or at school). Adults are often reluctant to encourage the child to talk about fears and anxieties. They believe that this will only increase the fears and anxieties. Also, parents may feel helpless in reassuring the child, and may be afraid of actually harming the child by continued discussions. Statements like, "I know you are afraid," or, "it is a scary feeling," are helpful and should be used. Being told it is normal and natural to be afraid is also reassuring.

A child's fears do not need to completely disrupt his and the family's activities.

It is apparent that there will be important concerns and things to do after a disaster: checking on the damage, cleaning up broken glass or fallen furniture. A child can and should be included in these activities. It is actually reassuring for a child if he is involved with the parent in these jobs. It is reassuring to see progress being made in bringing the house back to order and the routine of the household resumed: meals prepared, dishes washed, beds made, playmates coming over. For the parents of a very young child, the task is more difficult. Such a child may need more physical care, more holding; and this makes it harder for parents to attend to the other things that should be done. Unfortunately, there is no short-cut. If the child's needs are not met, the problem will persist for a longer period.

SETTLING DOWN

When things begin to settle down, after the "excitement" of the event has passed, some degree of lethargy may set in for both the parents and children. It is very important that parents make a deliberate effort to avoid inactivity and to get back to routine.

Parents should indicate to the child that they are maintaining control: they should be understanding but firm, supportive and make decisions for the child.

Parents may become appropriately more permissive, but discipline has to be maintained. If the family is evacuated, there will be a delay in a return to normal. Planned activities in such centers will increase the morale of all and prevent immobilization of the child's own resources.

BEDTIME PROBLEMS

The most frequently reported problem that parents encounter with their children occurs at bedtime.

The child may refuse to go to his room to sleep by himself. When he does go to bed, he may have difficulty falling asleep. He may wake up often during the night; he may have nightmares.

Parents question if they should make changes. Should they allow the child to sleep in the parents' bed, or in their bedroom or in another child's bed, or should the parent sleep in their child's room? It is necessary to become somewhat flexible. Bedtime may be delayed when the child is more anxious or wants to talk longer, but a limit should be set.

It is natural for a child to want to be close to his parents, and for the parents to want to have the child near them.

Some children, who are more anxious than others, can be allowed to move into a room with another child, or sleep on a mattress in the parents' bedroom. For another child it may be sufficient for the parent, at bedtime, to spend a little extra time in the child's bedroom reassuring him. All such arrangements, however, should return to normal after a few days. The parents and the child together should agree on the day for the return to his own bed (ideally not longer than 3-4 days hence) and the parents should abide by the decision. It is important for the child's independence that the parent be firm about his commitment.

Parents should also be aware of their own fears and their own uncertainty and of the effect these have upon the child.

If parents question – Is it going to be safe there? Will he be frightened? – they contribute to the child's continuing fear and his inability to go back to his room. Reassurance with firmness is an effective approach. Getting angry at the child, punishing, spanking, or shouting at him will rarely help. If the child comes out of his room calmly return him to it and reassure him of your presence nearby. It may be helpful to leave a nightlight on in the room, or in the hall, and leave his door ajar. Spending more time with the child during the day will make him feel more secure in the evening and at night.

SPECIFIC FEARS

Following a traumatic event, such as a natural disaster, irrational fears may develop in which some particular thing or situation evokes great anxiety to the point of panic, and is, therefore, strongly avoided. The child may become afraid of beds, his house, or darkness. A younger child may be afraid to go to school or even to leave his home. Reassurance to the younger child regarding monsters can be done by words, explanations, pointing out to the child the difference between his fantasy and reality. With school phobias (refusal to go to school), it is essential to see to it that the child gets to school. In this instance, firmness is necessary and the child should know that you expect him to attend school. The teacher or the school counselor can be of help to you.

REGRESSIVE BEHAVIOR

A child may sometimes revert to "childish" behavior which he has outgrown. Wetting his bed, clinging to the parents, thumb sucking, and other problems may occur temporarily, and should not alarm parents. They are normally of short duration. These behaviors are only signs of the child's anxiety, and parents' acceptance will reassure the child and shorten the duration of such behaviors. When parents over-react to these behavior patterns (become over-concerned, punish, or nag the child) these symptoms will persist much longer.

Children respond to praise, and parents should make a deliberate effort not to focus upon the child's immature behavior.

HOW CAN THE PARENTS RECOGNIZE WHEN TO SEEK PROFESSIONAL HELP?

Most parents are capable of helping their child overcome fears and anxiety. However, it is not a sign of failure if the parents find that they are unable to help their child by themselves. A telephone call to a pediatrician, family physician, the local mental health center or clinic could be helpful. In some cases, advice can be given on the telephone. In other instances, parents will be counseled to bring their child for an interview. In cases of severe anxiety, early action will result in a return to normal. Parents will recognize rather soon whether or not their attempts to help their child have been successful.

If the sleeping problem continues for more than a few nights, if the clinging behavior does not diminish, if the fears become worse, it is time to ask for professional advice.

Mental health professional are specially trained to help people in distress. They can help parents cope with and understand the unusual reactions of their child. By talking to the parents and child either individually or in groups, a child's fears can be overcome more easily.

Some parents are reluctant to consider seeking the help of a mental health professional or a clinic. However, more and more people are becoming aware that there is no stigma attached to seeking help. It is a way to avoid severe problems.

This manuscript was developed by the San Fernando Valley Child Guidance Clinic, 9650 Zelzah Avenue, Northridge, California 91325. No portion of this pamphlet may be reprinted or reproduced without permission from the San Fernando Valley Child Guidance Clinic.

APPENDIX II

EARTHQUAKES IN COASTAL BRITISH COLUMBIA

Coastal British Columbia at first glance looks more substantial than most landscapes. A rampart of mountains surrounds Vancouver, Vancouver Island has a snow-clad spine of mountains, and Victoria sprawls among glacier-scoured outcrops. It looks rock solid, but looks can be deceiving. Tens of kilometres beneath the surface, rock is anything but solid.

The earth's crust floats on a plastic-like mantle in vast plates that underlie the continents. These plates are in constant slow motion. Where they grind together their pressure shapes new mountain ranges. Where they pull apart they form sea troughs. The Pacific Rim's "ring of fire" contains many plates in several subduction zones. The steady collision of the plates produces dramatic upheavals in the earth's crust which sometimes become visible in the form of volcanic action, destructive water waves and several kinds of earthquake.

Deep under southwestern British Columbia, its offshore islands and waters, three large plates come together in a ragged jigsaw puzzle. The Pacific, Juan de Fuca and North America Plates together make up the Cascadia Subduction Zone which stretches from north of the Queen Charlotte Islands to the Oregon coast. The continental North America Plate moves westward, overriding the Juan de Fuca Plate, which subducts (slides under) eastward at a steady 4.3 centimetres a year. A fourth small plate, the Explorer Plate, also moves independently. The offshore Pacific Plate moves westward from the Juan de Fuca Ridge about 150 kilometres west of Vancouver Island. Here molten new plate material wells upward from deep in the earth's crust, causing the sea floor to spread and lift, and feeding volcanic mountains including Mount Garibaldi and the Cascade Range.

Plates can subduct smoothly in aseismic creep, causing little disruption and no earthquakes. For years many seismologists believed this was happening in the Cascadia zone, since it would explain the absence of major earthquakes over the last century.

New information from studies in Washington, Oregon and British Columbia leads many scientists to believe that the plates are not moving smoothly, but are temporarily locked in a strain accumulation phase. Their apparent inability to move further causes the earth's crust to measurably bulge upward – especially in a north-south corridor from Washington State's Olympic Peninsula to Campbell River – and builds enormous pressure. If coastal British Columbia and neighbouring states are indeed in a strain accumulation phase, this strain must eventually release as a great earthquake.

All earthquakes are related in some way to crustal movement and pressure, but the specific causes differ from area to area and from quake to quake. A strike-slip earthquake results from sideways motion along breaks or faults in the earth's crust such as California's San Andreas Fault and New Zealand's Alpine Fault. The 15-second 1989 Loma Prieta quake (Richter 7.1) was a strike-slip quake on the San Andreas Fault. Some faults extend from deep underground right up to the surface, where they may be visible in broken soil and rock layers. Coastal British Columbia has few surface faults, but can still experience powerful shallow quakes. In 1946, a strike-slip earthquake originating near Courtenay caused one death and widespread damage on Vancouver Island. The important Beaufort Fault lies not far away, near Comox Lake.

The devastating 1988 earthquake in northwest Armenia which killed more than 55,000 people was a thrust earthquake in which one section of land was violently pushed upward along a fault.

A truly cataclysmic subduction earthquake can result from the jolting loose of locked tectonic plates. The three-minute 1985 Mexico City quake, a subduction quake, may be a close analogy to The Big One expected in coastal British Columbia. It originated at the edge of the Cocos Plate off Mexico's west coast ، a young oceanic plate, like our Juan de Fuca Plate, which had been seismically quiet for many years ، yet it caused considerable damage in Mexico City more than 300 kilometres away, roughly as far from the coast as Vancouver is from Kamloops. It killed more than 9,000 people, left about 200,000 homeless and caused damage worth billions of dollars.

A team of Canadian seismologists and engineers which studied the Mexican quake returned with sombre warnings and recommendations for Western Canada. Some of its findings were incorporated into a significantly upgraded revision of the National Building Code of Canada. Other findings have spurred research into crustal movements in the Cascadia Subduction Zone.

"The 1985 earthquake occurred in a region where subduction could have been argued to be aseismic because of historical quiescence, but in retrospect, there was a seismic gap," (a temporarily inactive region where violent seismic activity could be expected soon), says the team's report, Lessons from the 1985 Mexican earthquake. "Until recently, some have argued that subduction beneath the Pacific Northwest is also occurring aseismically. This view may now need revision, and an earthquake off the coast of British Columbia of a magnitude similar to that of the Mexican earthquake cannot be excluded."

Government and business have not yet widely followed some of the team's recommendations, especially for bringing older structures up to a minimum standard of seismic building safety.

Coastal British Columbia has gone without a powerful subduction quake for several centuries, probably for about 300 years if we can judge by findings in Washington State. United States Geological Survey seismologist Dr. Brian Atwater has charted at least six major earthquakes in the last 3,500 years by studying soil layers and submerged forests. These point to sudden uplift and subsidence of coastal areas caused by great quakes. Most seismologists place the irregular interval between huge subduction quakes in this area at roughly 500 years.

A megaquake in British Columbia may be likely, but remains virtually unpredictable. In California small and large earthquakes are sufficiently frequent, their surface manifestations are sufficiently visible, and the recorded history is sufficiently long, that seismologists have a reasonably good idea of what to expect next. A pattern has emerged of quakes predicted at intervals of 21 to 303 years in different parts of the state, with reasonable estimates of probable magnitude.

Even in California prediction not yet possible. The 1989 Loma Prieta earthquake, for example, was loosely preceded by moderate foreshocks two and 15 months earlier in the Loma Prieta seismic gap. But the Loma Prieta quake occurred two months after the last foreshock, not a few days after, as the California Office of Emergency Services warned in a public advisory. As a result, Loma Prieta confirmed seismologists' long-term suspicions but gave the general public no real warning. Research is steadily improving the odds, but it may be years before scientists can confidently issue a realistic earthquake alert. The People's Republic of China, which studies earthquake prediction intensively and has issued full-scale alerts sending thousands of people from their homes and workplaces, failed to predict the catastrophic 1976 Tangshan quake which killed about 242,000 people.

Canada has recently pursued earthquake research for coastal British Columbia, the aseismic intervals are long, the probable locations are remote and invisible, and the quakes appear to be potentially gigantic. As a result, we are still trying to develop a probability pattern like the one developed for California.

Severity of The Big One will depend mainly on its hypocentre or focus and on its duration, which in turn will depend on whether it is a strike-slip or subduction quake. The first phase of the Greater Vancouver Regional District's damage prediction study considers the dual possibility of a 7.5 Richter strike-slip quake in the Gulf Islands and a maximum 9.2 Richter subduction quake off the west coast of Vancouver Island. A 7.5 quake, a little stronger than the quake that caused such widespread damage in sparsely populated areas of Vancouver Island in 1946, would be of shocking severity today in densely populated southern Vancouver Island and the Lower Mainland. A 9.2 quake probably would produce less violent shaking in Vancouver because of its distance. Dr. Weichert says the length of the section of the subduction zone that ruptures, releasing its accumulated strain, will determine magnitude. The Cascadia zone runs from northern Vancouver Island to California, but may be broken by several east-west faults. Different sections could rupture in sequence, producing milder shaking than a single rupture along the entire zone.

"But even if it does rupture in three phases we will still have three magnitude eights, on that order," Weichert says. "If the whole thing unzips in one, then it's a magnitude nine, perhaps, even nine point two."

Extent of damage is no easier to foresee than other aspects. Hazard assessment reports prepared for Vancouver and Richmond, a brief by the Association of Professional Engineers of British Columbia, and several other studies all mention several prime concerns: liquefaction of landfill, alluvial and other soft soils; resonance in various soil types and structures; damage to sea defences including sea dykes; and damage caused by tidal waves or tsunamis. Together these could create landslides, surface fissures, slumping, fire and flooding. These in turn could cause severe damage to buildings, transportation networks, utilities and communications.

Awareness is also growing about possible uplift and subsidence, based on effects of subduction earthquakes elsewhere on North and South America's west coast, particularly the 1960 Chilean quake (9.5 magnitude) and the 1985 Mexican quake (8.1 magnitude). These indicate that a great quake might cause subsi-

Tsunamis usually produce a series of giant waves. The tsunami generated by the 1964 earthquake stranded boats and caused heavy property damage at Seaward, Alaska. Waves destroyed railway docks, washed out tracks and bridges, and hurled cars and railway rolling stock into jumbled heaps. They also spread burning petroleum over the waterfront, igniting the wreckage and many buildings.

dence on southern Vancouver Island, Washington and northern Oregon, and uplift north of central Vancouver Island.

These possibilities – and they are only possibilities – await coastal British Columbia. Heritage neighbourhoods of Vancouver, Victoria, New Westminster and Nanaimo could suffer widespread building damage. Liquefaction could damage buildings, roads and other structures in landfill areas of Campbell River, Richmond, Victoria and Vancouver. Fraser River and Fraser Delta areas could experience waterfront slumping, disruption of several airports, and failure of sea and river containment dykes. North and West Vancouver could suffer landslides and failure of dams and reservoirs. Tsunami and flood damage could affect coastal areas. Throughout coastal British Columbia, failure of commercial and residential buildings could cause injuries, both physical and psychological, and deaths. We can only hope never to experience these worst-case scenarios.

TSUNAMI

A tidal wave or tsunami (the word means harbour wave in Japanese) often follows an underwater earthquake, but whether coastal British Columbia will experience this depends on the earthquake's epicentre and strength.

Most emergency planners don't consider tsunamis to be a major threat in the Inside Passage, Gulf Islands or coastal mainland of British Columbia after a quake nearby. Destructive waves in lakes and ocean drowned one man and caused some damage ashore in the 1946 Vancouver Island earthquake; they resulted not from a tsunami but from submarine slumping and landslides. The coast could also receive powerful waves arriving from Japan, Hawaii, Alaska or elsewhere on the Pacific Rim, with considerable destructive potential.

The 1964 Alaska earthquake (9.2 magnitude) generated waves that killed more people than the actual quake, including a majority of the 131 Alaska victims and 13 people swept away in coastal Crescent City, California. Waves caused considerable damage on the west coast of Vancouver Island. The tsunami struck Tofino as a 2.6 metre wave and, after surging up the Alberni Inlet, struck Port Alberni as a wave of more than four metres. The first wave put the tide gauge out of commission; the second and third waves may have reached a height of 4.5 metres. The waves caused an estimated $10 million damage in Port Alberni. Residents received no warning because a year earlier the federal government had pulled out of an international tsunami watch system based in Hawaii, which it has since rejoined. Miraculously, there were no deaths.

A 1990 study by British Columbia oceanographers Paul LeBlond, Tad Murty and Max Ng suggested that an earthquake in the Cascadia Subduction Zone west of Vancouver Island could generate waves of up to 16 metres at Port Alberni at the head of the Alberni Inlet, which would amplify the tsunami. Other west coast areas could receive five-metre waves. The tsunami could produce waves of up to two metres at Victoria, and up to one metre at Vancouver, Richmond and Delta. A one-metre wave at high tide could cause serious flooding.

SCALES OF MAGNITUDE

The most familiar measurement of earthquakes is the Richter scale of magnitude, developed by Dr. C.F. Richter. The scale is logarithmic; each one-point increase in magnitude represents a tenfold increase in earthquake size and about a 30-fold increase in energy. The Richter scale measures intensity only at the earthquake epicentre. Some typical Richter observations:

R1-R4.9	may be felt; no damage
R5-R5.9	moderate damage possible
R6-R7.4	major damage possible
R7.5-R9+	a great quake; severe damage possible

The Modified Mercalli intensity scale measures the degree of shaking felt in various locations, based on observations of damage and effects on people. It is usually highest at the epicentre and drops with distance; a Modified Mercalli map usually shows intensity in concentric gradations diminishing outward from the epicentre. Accurate widespread observation is required for this measurement. Modified Mercalli intensities are written in Roman numerals. Some excerpts:

I	not felt
II	felt by people at rest
III	felt indoors; hanging objects swing; light vibration
IV	heavy vibration; windows and dishes rattle
V	felt outdoors; sleepers awaken; doors swing open or closed
VI	felt by all; many people frightened; plaster and masonry may crack; glass and crockery break; furniture moves or overturns
VII	difficult to stand; waves on ponds; ornamental masonry falls
VIII	considerable building damage; difficult to steer cars; tree branches break
IX	general panic; unbolted buildings shift off foundations; underground pipes break; conspicuous cracks in ground; sandboils
X	most masonry and frame structures destroyed; serious damage to well-built structures; serious damage to dams; large landslides
XI	rails bend; underground pipes completely out of service
XII	damage nearly total; objects thrown into the air

Another classification used mainly by seismologists is Moment Magnitude, or energy magniture, which is based on the amount of energy released by an earthquake. This is the most accurate magnitude scale, but it is more difficult to calculate than other scales.

SOME MAJOR EARTHQUAKES IN BRITISH COLUMBIA MEASURED ON RICHTER SCALE

1872	Northern Washington	7+
1909	Gulf Islands	6
1910	Queen Charlottes	6.8
1918	Vancouver Island	7
1918	Revelstoke	6
1920	Gulf Islands	5.5
1929	Queen Charlottes	7
1946	Courtenay	7.3
1949	Queen Charlottes	8.1
1970	Queen Charlottes	7.4
1976	Pender Island	5.4

MAJOR QUAKES WORLDWIDE MEASURED IN MOMENT MAGNITUDE

1755	Lisbon, Portugal	8.7	60,000 deaths
1811-2	New Madrid, Missouri	8.7	no deaths
1906	San Francisco	7.9	503 deaths
	(doubtful official count)		
1906	Valparaiso, Chile	8.2	20,000 deaths
1923	Yokohama	7.9	200,000 deaths
1927	Nan-Shan, China	7.6	200,000 deaths
1933	Japan	8.4	2,990 deaths
1960	Southern Chile	9.5	5,000 deaths
1964	Alaska	9.2	131 deaths
1976	Guatemala	7.5	22,778 deaths
1976	Tangshan, China	7.5	242,000 deaths
1985	Mexico City	8.1	9,000-plus deaths
1988	Northwest Armenia	6.8	55,000-plus deaths
1989	Loma Prieta, Calif.	7.0	63 deaths

QUAKE CHECKLIST

GO BAG

Lightweight, compact, easy to carry in one hand or over your shoulder, containing only the essentials: keep these characteristics in mind as you compile your go bag. A cheap nylon day pack or tote bag makes a good container. Here are some useful contents:

- small first aid kit with instruction booklet
- flashlight and spare batteries
- radio and spare batteries
- ready to eat food and drink (juice pack and granola or candy bar) for the family
- canned or bottled water in an easy-to-carry size
- water purification tablets
- manual can-opener
- a week's prescription medication for all family members (recycle regularly to keep fresh)
- basic medical needs for the bedridden or ill
- spare eyeglasses for all family members
- baby food or infant formula (even if you breastfeed)
- baby supplies including disposable diapers, moist towelettes, diaper rash cream
- change of underwear, also a change of clothes if space permits
- comfortable old shoes
- space blanket
- plastic poncho
- toiletry items
- identification and important papers
- photos of all family members
- cash, including quarters for pay phone
- phone number of out-of-province contact person
- several large and small plastic garbage bags

Add personal items to your go bag as needed. I sometimes keep my computer backup disks there. Paper and pencil, a book, and a deck of cards don't take much space but could help you endure the anxious hours in a reception centre.

QUAKE KIT FOR BABIES

Store a week's worth of baby or infant supplies in your home earthquake kit:
- blankets
- changes of clothes
- disposable diapers (you won't have enough water to safely wash cloth diapers)
- moist towelettes
- food
- formula (even if you breastfeed; you may be injured, absent or unable to nurse your baby)
- bottles with disposable liners; some ready-to-use formula is available in disposable bottles with disposable nipples
- powdered or canned milk
- a bottle or two of Pedialyte or another fluid-replacement liquid
- teether or pacifier
- baby soap
- diaper rash cream
- baby aspirin or Tempra
- thermometer
- week's supply of any prescription medicine
- duplicate of a favourite toy or cuddly

Recycle all these items often. Babies grow quickly; newborn-size diapers and infant formula won't be any use to a toddler.

HOME FIRST AID KIT

Your home first aid kit should contain as a minimum:
- first aid handbook
- roll of adhesive tape, 7.5 centimetres by five metres
- two sterile gauze bandages, 7.5 centimetres by 7.5 centimetres
- band aids, box of assorted sizes
- 10 antiseptic swabs
- elastic bandage, 7.5 centimetres by five metres
- two large burn pads
- two pressure pads, 20 centimetres by 20 centimetres
- six triangular bandages (slings)
- thermometer with case
- lunt-point bandage scissors
- sharp-point bandage scissors

- tweezers with long points
- tube of eye ointment
- tube of zinc oxide ointment
- calamine lotion in plastic bottle
- 50 painkiller tablets
- 25 anti-nausea tablets
- a week's supply of prescription medicines
- spare eyeglasses

You could also add:
- tube of petroleum jelly
- package of safety pins, assorted sizes
- pocket flashlight with batteries
- instant hot and cold compress
- plastic bags
- candles and matches
- disposable hand wipes
- two foil space blanket
- needle
- ammonia inhalant
- moleskin (hikers' blister-prevention adhesive)

PET QUAKE KIT
A pet emergency kit should include:
- pet first aid kit
- at least three days' supply of food and water; recycle regularly
- can opener, water dish, paper plates
- blanket and towels
- collar, leash and identification tags
- paper towels and plastic bags for cleanup
- travel kennel
- health and vaccination records
- medications with instructions
- veterinarian's name and phone number

A pet first aid kit will treat minor injuries until you can get your pet to a veterinarian. Vancouver SPCA sells a modestly-priced pet first aid kit which includes:
- roll of gauze bandage, five centimetres
- roll of gauze bandage, 2.5 centimetres
- roll of adhesive tape, 2.5 centimetres

- roll of cotton batting, five centimetres
- four gauze bandages, 10 centimetres by 10 centimetres
- four gauze bandages, five centimetres by five centimetres
- six Q-tips
- four tongue depressors to use as splints
- Kaopectate to coat and protect intestines against diarrhea and poisons
- Betadine solution, a bland iodine disinfectant for skin and wounds (not eyes)
- three per cent hydrogen peroxide to induce vomiting or disinfect skin and wounds
- antibiotic eye ointment
- scissors
- tweezers

EARTHQUAKE RESPONSE FLOOR PLAN

Your earthquake response floor plan should show:
- fire extinguishers
- shut-offs for gas, electricity and water
- any potential structural or fire hazards
- safest places in each room for riding out an earthquake
- main exit from each room
- second emergency exit from each room
- emergency exit equipment, for example, rope ladder
- go bag
- emergency supplies
- first aid kit

Note this information below the sketch:
- reunion places for family members if separated; give at least one
- alternative
- name and phone number of out-of-province contact person
- date you made the sketch

BEFORE THE QUAKE HITS

Your plan will be as individual as your family, but here are some suggested pre-earthquake tasks:
- lead a home hazard hunt, and correct any problems
- check household insurance policy for earthquake coverage, and upgrade if necessary
- arrange for writing or revising of will

- copy important documents and place copies in
  safe deposit box or fireproof strongbox
- compile photos of family members and pets
- photograph or videotape home room by
  room for household inventory
- collect spare eyeglasses and week's supply
  of medication for each family member
- collect week's supply of drinking water
- collect emergency food supplies
- collect emergency camping supplies including
  sanitation needs
- collect emergency repair materials and tools
- collect and place wrenches and other tools for
  shutting off utility service
- stay in your building at least another 10 minutes
  to wait for immediate aftershocks

WHEN THE GROUND STARTS SHAKING

- Stay calm; don't shout or run around,
  which will upset you and other people
- stay where you are; move to a safe spot you've identified
- don't rush outside while the ground is shaking;
  this is extremely dangerous
- move away from windows, mirrors,
  light fixtures, hanging plants and tall pieces of furniture
- find a desk, table or other sturdy piece of furniture
  to get under and then, duck, cover and hold
- if you can't get under a piece of furniture,
  brace yourself in a hallway or a doorway
  (taking care that the door can't slam on your hands),
- stand in a corner or flatten yourself against an inside wall
  and protect your head with anything you can grab
- watch for falling fixtures, ceilings, or objects
- identify the fastest and safest exit in case
  you need to escape quickly
- if you feel panicky, count, snap your fingers
  or give the earthquake a piece of your mind
- stay where you are for 60 seconds after the
  shaking stops before moving around
- stay in your building at least another 10 minutes
  to wait for immediate aftershocks

FURTHER READING

ARTICLES

Canby, Thomas Y. "California Earthquake – Prelude to the Big One?" *National Geographic*. Vol. 177, No. 5, May 1990.

Comerio, Mary. "The Quiet Loss." *Networks Emergency Preparedness News*. Vol. 5, No. 1, Winter 1990.

Cooper, F.D. "The Prediction No One Wants to Hear: the great Quake." *Emergency Preparedness Digest*. Vol. 14, No. 4, October-December 1987.

Dragert, H., and G.C. Rogers. "Could a megathrust earthquake strike southwestern British Columbia?" *Geos*. Vol. 3, 1988.

"The Economics of Earthquakes." An interview with Dr. Charles Thiel. *Networks Emergency Preparedness News*. Special Report, undated.

Fain, Linda F., and Diane Myers. "Emotional Aftershocks." *Networks Emergency Preparedness News*. Vol. 5, No. 1, Winter 1990.

Frantz, Thomas T. "Post-Traumatic Stress in the Classroom." Excerpted from paper. *Networks Emergency Preparedness News*. Vol. 4, No. 3, Fall 1989.

Hill, Rev. John. "`Haven't You Got Over It Yet?' The Complexities of Disaster Recovery." *Networks Emergency Preparedness News*. Vol. 5, No. 1, Winter 1990.

Hodgson, Ernest A. "British Columbia Earthquake, June 23, 1946." *Journal of the Royal Astronomical Society of Canada*. 1946.

Howard, Stephen J. "Children and the San Fernando earthquake." *Earthquake Information Bulletin*. Vol. 12, No. 5, September-October 1980.

Koppel, Tom. "Earthquake! Major quake overdue on the West Coast." *Canadian Geographic*. August-September 1989.

Lafond, Raymond. "Emergency Planning for the Elderly." *Emergency Preparedness Digest*. Vol. 14, No. 3, July-September 1987.

Mitchell, Denis, et al. "Lessons from the 1985 Mexican earthquake." *Canadian Journal of Civil Engineering*. Vol. 13, 1986.

O'Callahan, Bill. "Post-Earthquake Stress: Seismic Strain on Human Psyche." *Networks Emergency Preparedness News*. Vol. 3, No. 1, Fall-Winter 1987-88.

Plafker, George, and John P. Galloway, editors. "Lessons learned from the Loma Prieta, California, Earthquake of October 17, 1989." *U.S. Geological Survey*. Circular 1045.

Rapaport, Richard. "Shakedown for the Media." *Networks Emergency Preparedness News*. Vol. 5, No. 1, Winter 1990.

Renteria, Henry. "When the Going Got Tough." *Networks Emergency Preparedness News*. Vol. 5, No. 1, Winter 1990.

Rogers, Garry C. and Henry S. Hasegawa. "A Second Look at the British Columbia Earthquake of June 23, 1946." *Bulletin of the Seismological Society of America*. Vol. 68, No. 3, June 1978.

Savage, J.C. and M. Lisowski. "Strain Measurements and the Potential for a Great Subduction Earthquake Off the Coast of Washington." *Science*. Vol. 252, April 1991.

Sunset's guide to help you prepare for the next quake. *Sunset Magazine*, October 1990.

"Taking Care of Business." *Networks Earthquake Preparedness News*. Vol. 4, No. 2, Summer 1989.

Tempelman-Kluit, Anne. "Countdown to Cataclysm." *Equinox*. No. 47, September-October 1989.

Ward, Peter L. and Robert A. Page. "The Loma Prieta Earthquake of October 17, 1989." *Earthquakes & Volcanoes*. Vol. 21, No. 6, 1989.

BOOKS

The assessment and mitigation of earthquake risk. Paris: The United Nations, 1978.

Gere, James M., and Haresh C. Shah. *Terra Non Firma*. New York: W.H. Freeman and Company, 1984.

Heppenheimer, T.A. *The Coming Quake*. New York: Times Books, 1988.

Kimball, Virginia. *Earthquake Ready*. Santa Monica: Roundtable Publishing, 1988.

Lafferty, Libby. *Earthquake Preparedness*. La Canada, California: Lafferty & Associates, Inc., 1989.

McCann, John P. *How to Prepare for an Earthquake*. New York: Insurance Information Institute, 1985.

News staff of the San Francisco Chronicle. *The Quake of '89*. San Francisco: Chronicle Books, 1989.

Page, Robert A., and Peter W. Basham. *Earthquake Hazards in the Offshore Environment*. U.S. Geological Survey Bulletin 1630. Washington: Department of the Interior and U.S. Geological Survey, 1985.

Registration and Inquiry Manual. Ottawa: Health and Welfare Canada, 1986.

Reitherman, Robert. *Reducing The Risks Of Nonstructural Earthquake Damage: A Practical Guide*. Oakland: Bay Area Regional Earthquake Preparedness Project, second edition, October 1985.

Seismic Risk in British Columbia: 1988 Brief to the British Columbia Government. Vancouver: Association of Professional Engineers of British Columbia, 1988.

Scott, Stanley. *Policies for Seismic Safety: Elements of a State Governmental Program*. Berkeley: Institute of Governmental Studies, 1979.

van Rose, Susannah. *Earthquakes*. London: Geological Museum, 1983.

NEWSPAPERS AND PERIODICALS

Vancouver *Province*
Vancouver *Sun*
Daily Times-Colonist, Victoria
Emergency Preparedness Digest.

NETWORKS: Earthquake Preparedness News. Bay Area Regional Earthquake Preparedness Project. Vols. 1 (1985) to 6 (1991).

PAMPHLETS AND FACT SHEETS

Are you prepared in case of disaster? Ottawa: Health and Welfare Canada, 1988.

Be Prepared! a Check List of Emergency Supplies. Victoria: British Columbia Provincial Emergency Program, undated.

A Blueprint for Earthquake Survival. Saanich: Saanich Emergency Program, undated.

Coping with Children's Reactions to Earthquakes and Other Disasters. Northridge, California: San Fernando Valley Child Guidance Clinic, 1986.

The Earthquake Business Plan: A Planning Guide for Commercial Organisations. Wellington: New Zealand Ministry of Civil Defence, 1990.

The Earthquake Business Plan: A Planning Guide for Corporate Organisations. Wellington: New Zealand Ministry of Civil Defence, 1990.

The Earthquake Business Plan: A Planning Guide for Small Business. Wellington: New Zealand Ministry of Civil Defence, 1990.

Earthquake Preparedness Activities for Child Care Providers. Oakland: Bay Area Regional Earthquake Preparedness Project, April 1988.

Earthquake Preparedness: A Key to Small Business Survival. Oakland: Bay Area Regional Earthquake Preparedness Project, undated.

Earthquake Preparedness: Highrises – Mobile Homes. Ottawa: Emergency Preparedness Canada, May 1990.

Earthquake Preparedness: People with Disabilities. Ottawa: Emergency Preparedness Canada, May 1990.

Earthquake Safety Checklist. San Francisco: Federal Emergency Management Agency, October 1985.

FURTHER READING

Emergency Planning for Your Pet. Vancouver: Western Federation of Individuals and Dog Organizations, undated.

Emergency Preparedness in Canada. Ottawa: Emergency Preparedness Canada, 1987.

Family Earthquake Drill. San Francisco: Federal Emergency Management Agency, September 1983.

Family Preparedness for Earthquakes and Other Emergencies. Ottawa: Emergency Preparedness Canada, undated.

Geofacts: Seismic Hazard Calculation. Ottawa: Energy, Mines and Resources Canada, March 1990.

A Guide for the Homeowner to Repair, Alter, Add to or Construct a One or Two Family Dwelling, etc. Richmond: City of Richmond, January 1990.

Home buyer's guide to earthquake hazards. Oakland: Bay Area Regional Earthquake Preparedness Project, undated.

Home Hazard Hunt. San Francisco: Federal Emergency Management Agency, September 1983.

In an Emergency: Earthquake. Richmond: Corporation of Richmond, undated.

Learning to Live in Earthquake Country: Preparedness for People with Disabilities. Oakland: Bay Area Regional Earthquake Preparedness Project, October 1985.

Learning to Live in Earthquake Country: Preparedness in Apartments and Mobile Homes. Oakland: Bay Area Regional Earthquake Preparedness Project, October 1985.

The Next Big Earthquake. Menlo Park, California: United States Geological Survey, undated.

Prepare now for an earthquake in British Columbia. Vancouver: Insurance Bureau of Canada, 1991.

Retrofit Before a Quake. Richmond: City of Richmond, undated.

School Earthquake Safety Guidebook. Victoria: British Columbia Ministry of Education, September 1987.

Strengthening wood frame houses for earthquake safety. Oakland: Bay Area Regional Earthquake Preparedness Project, undated.

What We Have Done to be Prepared for a Catastrophic Earthquake. Ottawa: Emergency Preparedness Canada, May 1990.

Yogi's Bear Facts: Earthquake Preparedness. Los Angeles: Hanna-Barbera Productions, Inc., undated.

PAPERS AND REPORTS

City of Richmond. *Earthquakes.* Report to council, 1990.

Commission for the Prevention of Violence Against Women. *Violence Against Women in the Aftermath of the October 17, 1989 Earthquake.* Santa Cruz: Report to Santa Cruz Mayor and City Council, 1990.

Lloyd, Brad. *The Plate Tectonic Setting of British Columbia: Its Geological Implications.* Unpublished paper, 1990.

Provincial Emergency Program. *1990 Report on Government Earthquake Preparedness Initiatives.* British Columbia Ministry of Solicitor General report, 1990.

Robinson Dames & Moore. *Greater Vancouver Regional District Earthquake Damage Prediction Study.* Phase I Preliminary Report, 1988.

VIDEOTAPE

Surviving the Big One: How to Prepare for a Major Earthquake. Los Angeles: Los Angeles City Fire Department and KCET Video, 1989.

Quake of '89: A Video Chronicle. San Francisco: KRON-TV, 1989.

INDEX